It is raining, hard. Picture a man, driving home from work, barely able to make out the road ahead. The tires slide and just like that, he flashes back to a time he would rather not recall.

On that cruel day, it was a Wednesday, the 30th of August. He was in a work meeting and received a phone call. Instead of screening the typical student loan relief, home security alarm, or politician's robocall, the caller ID said it was his wife. She never called him at work. She always texted instead. He answered. It wasn't her voice on the other end.

A co-worker explained his wife had fainted. She was coming to consciousness. An ambulance was on the way. Then, his wife appeared on the phone.

They spoke only briefly. She was thinking clearly.

"I guess I fainted," she said. "I'm fine. Everyone is making a big deal. They called for an ambulance."

She told him, "you need to go get Madison."

He had to meet their daughter's bus at home and he had to hurry to get there in time. He told her he loved her, and the line went dead. He assumed she would be fine.

Those were the final words she ever spoke.

As he drove home – to meet the bus which turned out to be her final wish – a tropical storm dumped rain on his commute. He cursed the standing highway water that had his car slipping and sliding as he hurried south.

His wife's co-worker called back to explain the ambulance took her to Thomas Hospital in Fairhope, about ten miles south of her workplace and over an hour away from his. Just before she ended the call, she told him to hurry.

He thought it odd at the time, but it foreshadowed the beginning of the worst moment of his life. He had no idea what was coming.

He made it home just ahead of the bus, collected his daughter and headed to the emergency room. He parked in a soggy spot in the corner and walked into the ER with his daughter in tow. He told the receptionist who he was and who he was there to see. She looked at him seriously and despite her best intentions, her eyes betrayed her. More foreshadowing – so evident in hindsight.

They were escorted to a waiting room where a lady came in to sit with them. A few minutes later, a doctor came in.

"I don't know what they have told you," he said directly.

"Not much, just that she fainted at work and was brought here."

"Well, it is more than that," the doctor explained. "She came in with cardiac arrest. She was revived multiple times in the ambulance on the way here. We worked on her for a long time, over thirty minutes. We were unable to resuscitate her, and she expired."

Those words wash over him. So much to absorb. His heart races as he cannot process what was just said.

"We were unable to resuscitate her." Those six words replay in his mind and would continue to do so for a long, long time.

"She's dead? What the Hell? Oh my God!"

The doctor explained more things that the man later wishes he could remember. He doesn't. One never knows how they will respond when their world shatters.

He didn't cry. Tears would come later. He was in disbelief. He was confused. Shock might be the appropriate word. With his face in his hands, he then remembered he was not alone in the waiting room.

"The girl over there," he points without looking up, "she has autism and her mom did everything for her. What are we going to do now?"

The flashback ends. The rain doesn't.

The following months after her passing, the man's life passed from rock-bottom despair, to overwhelming grief and uncertainty, to beating himself up over missed opportunities, to eventual acceptance of his situation. This tragic event smacked him out of his cruise-control life and pushed him into someone focused on being a better father and person. Sometimes, he succeeds. Other times, he falls on his face.

This is that journey. Raw, emotional, reflective, at times humorous and somber, but oh so real.

As his world crashed around him, Mark turned to writing as a way to organize the chaos. The story resonated with people and he kept sharing.

This book chronicles many of those posts along with other content never shared publicly. Follow along with good days and bad, laughter and tears, along with many more stories about the challenges for a recent widower facing grief in a unique setting. The stories range from the events just before his wife's death and continue for the next year. The storylines deal with his struggles looking back at his relationship, day-to-day household management struggles, learning how to help his daughter with her own grief, a harsh introduction into single parenting and eventually his decision to wade into a strange dating world again after 26 years with one woman.

Through it all, his 18-year old daughter Madison is by his side. Labeled as non-verbal, her limited vocabulary and complicated worldview adds another challenge to the situation. How in the world will she get by without the mother who served as her lifeline?

All the tears. Every damn one.

But more follow.

It is 4:37 AM Friday morning. I haven't slept since Tuesday night. Because on Wednesday afternoon, Hannah - my wife of 22 years and mother of our 18-year-old daughter - died suddenly from cardiac arrest.

All the tears.

That kind of a blow shakes your core. So many questions. So many emotions. So much uncertainty.

Every time my eyes close, I think of Hannah and am wide awake.

Hannah wasn't always a great spouse. Then again, who is? She had her insecurities, her shortfalls and many have questioned her choice of a husband. But she was unequivocally, without question a loving mom.

Many have seen it but y'all just don't know the half of it.

Our daughter Madison has autism. Almost everything is harder for Madison than it is for you and me. Beyond what you see publicly, Hannah helped Madison with life. Showers, toiletry, feminine hygiene, digestive issues, leg shaving, texture issues, a fixation on hair, makeup, and that just gets us started.

Madison's dad is now tasked with supporting those activities and many more that will arrive as she ages. You do not want to see Dad's first day as a makeup artist.

Looking back, I wasn't as involved with assisting Hannah as I should have been. Many were unpleasant for me – as I'm sure they were for Hannah – and I was content letting her do them. She was better at it than me, so why not? I have to live with that fact – one among many regrets racing through the circuits on the sleepless nights.

So here we are. And of course, I am lost.

One of the most challenging parts of this week has been the lack of transition. When Hannah would go out of town and Madison stayed with her dad, she would prep on the do's and don'ts, and provide tips for how to avoid the pitfalls that the unaccustomed will stumble into with Madi.

I can't ask Hannah a lot of important things (like the username and passwords to all our online bill accounts), but I also can't get that reassurance that no, the toaster strudels can't be microwaved. They have to be oven-toasted on both sides for common intervals and then the frosting has to be smeared evenly over one side of the strudel.

And so, we learn. And we make mistakes. And hopefully learn more, faster than anyone ever learned anything before.

Friends and family have swooped in to do whatever they can do. We feel that support system. It would be unbearable without it this week … and for who knows how long?

Frankly, I didn't know I can be this distraught about anything. Just no context. It's raw. There's no "going through the motions" as most of us do the majority of our lives mindlessly clicking our phones or making small-talk. At this point I feel everything. Every comment, every familiar face walking forward with a bearhug and every memory makes me flare red hot.

I have to admit that there is nothing like death to make you feel alive. I don't want to feel this anymore. But this feeling isn't going anywhere.

All the tears.

The last few days have been a blur. I'm trying to focus on getting a plan in place for Madison, making sure she is aware of our new reality but also trying to reassure her I am up for this role. Meanwhile, we are making final arrangements for Hannah, fielding visits and messages and trying to somehow not start another sobbing episode.

At some point, I will have to make peace that my relationship with Hannah -- we have been together since she was 18, I was 19 -- is now something different. What it is, I don't really know. I'm still referring to her in present tense and stopping myself as I almost answer questions with, "Hannah will know."

I depended on her far more than I realized.

She was the strong one. She would have excelled getting Madison through this. That is the irony of it all.

All the tears.

The next time something happens that I get excited about, or irritated, or just something she would like – what do I do with that? Who do I share that with? She was my best friend and now I realize she knew way more about me than I did about her.

Yes, those regrets are piling up.

Oh, how I wish I could go back and do certain things differently. A word here. A gesture there. The little things that would have mattered to her that I just blatantly missed. I knew these things, but you know, I didn't prioritize them. Sometimes we get so wrapped up in achieving and collecting that we forget the reason we do all that stuff is the people that matter to us.

Hannah, I just wanted to make you proud of me. Like I am of the job you did as Madison's mom.

There were times I wasn't a particularly supportive husband. I was selfish and focused on my own interests and achievements often at your expense. I likely couldn't have made-that-right with her last week before her death. As it is now, I am just lost in my head playing the time machine what-if game.

So, all I know to do is emulate Hannah's relationship with Madison. Yes, I'm going to struggle with things she made look easy. I'm going to experience failures. Madison is going to wish her mom was here to not screw things up. I'm going to try to learn from those mis-steps and improve.

Hannah, my next batch of achievements will involve Madison. Just like yours.

Rest easy love, we got this.

Madison said her good-byes today.

Losing your mother has got to be one of the worst things imaginable. But imagine she has been your lifeline to the outside world – your caretaker, coach, translator, and best friend.

Hannah is being cremated Saturday. When she talked about death, which wasn't often, but in our quarter century spending almost every day together, it came up. It was her wish for everyone to not make a big fuss over her. She wanted no service, no pomp and circumstance, and really felt like she would be gone so just spread her ashes somewhere and be done with it. She was practical about it.

I think she underestimated how people felt about her. How her strength touched so many. How her easy smile disarmed people. She was easy to like, easy to love. She was mine for a while, but she belonged to you all. She just didn't know it.

Trying to plan funeral arrangements when your world has crashed around you – well, I am sure I messed something up. Trying to find a balance between how she viewed herself and how so many others saw her gave me pause. I wanted to please everyone. Do I follow her wishes? Or do I do what others expect?

However, this really should be about what is best for those closest to Hannah. And obviously, what is best for Madison should be a priority, as it always was for Hannah. Our girl has to be so confused about this week's events. Lord knows, her dad is.

I decided to aid Madison's understanding of this ordeal, we would have a private viewing at the funeral home. Like many of us, Madison is a visual learner. Allowing her to see what we have been persistently trying to explain would reinforce the stark reality and give us a glimpse to see how much she understands.

She is aware her mom is gone. Madison hasn't asked for her, which she would do if Hannah was away for a day or two. But right or wrong, this is another decision to make at a time when I'd rather be hiding under a bed.

We arrive at the funeral home and I explain my wishes for our schedule. People will cooperate if they know what you want. I'm seeing the best in humanity at the time it is needed the most, regardless of how our world is viewed on television.

We go through the plan. I will make the funeral arrangements while Hannah's family will sit in the lobby with Madison. Then I will have some time to visit with Hannah's body, before bringing Madison in with me. Then we will open up for her mother, brothers and the handful of others in the circle.

How will this go? Is this the right move? How will Madison react to seeing her mom, cold, lying on a table?

Hell, for that matter, how will any of us react? But that can't be the focus now. My girl has encountered so many obstacles in her life, we really have to maximize the best of the worst with this week's tragedy.

I keep thinking, "Isn't her life hard enough without this? Isn't her load heavy enough without removing her lifeline?"

But that just rips me up again and I'm no good to her or anyone. So, we regroup and take another step forward.

This will be the last time to see this girl who I spent decades trying to impress. She bought me a shirt recently and commented fondly each time I wore it. I wore it for her one last time. Why would I do that?

It seems silly in hindsight, but I just hoped to create one more smile. Unfortunately, some wishes will always remain wishes.

I finish the arrangements and I wait to see my wife's body.

Thankfully, someone in Hannah's family thought to call and ask the funeral home how she will be presented for our viewing. Due to the cremation, she isn't dressed for visitors. Just a sheet and no one wants that to be Madison's last image of her mother, so Hannah's mom brought a dress.

The funeral director and I make the long walk – how can only a few feet seem so far? I am left alone to approach. My wife isn't wearing makeup, her hair isn't fixed. Her autopsy scars peek out from under the dress. Her lip has a cut from the breathing tube. It is her ... but it isn't.

She doesn't notice my shirt.

She is gone. I don't know what I expect to get out of this meeting, but I have some words planned. Similar to a presentation for work, I know what I want to say, and I deliver it aloud to this body that a few days earlier had housed my world – the only girl I ever loved.

The words end. I reach out and touch her hand. The coldness stops me. I don't like it.

While the bulk of the message will always remain private, I will share one small piece. Hannah was always fascinated by ghosts. She went on ghost hunts and tours and had an app on her phone that tracked activity. I didn't share her affinity. There are so many things she liked I now wish I would've taken more interest in joining her. I dismissed too many of her passions and now desperately want a do-over.

I think someone used the word, torment. This is apt.

I talk about Madison, and how we are going to get through this. And how if Hannah wants to come back – however that works – we can use all the help we can find.

Earlier that day on the three-hour drive to the funeral home, I explain multiple times to Madison what we are doing. She receives as much prep as I am able to provide. She cries a few times. I take that as a sign the message is getting through.

God, I hope I am doing the right thing.

When we approach the body on the table, Madison isn't surprised by what she sees. She says, "Mommy. Gone."

And we talk.

About how her mom loved her more than anything in this world. About all of the good memories that will always make us happy. About how she took care of everyone. And that we can talk about her – and more importantly to her - anytime we want. And if you listen closely, you may get an answer.

As our conversation stalls, Madison reaches out and touches the arm on the table in front of her.

"Cold," she says, and takes a few steps backward. I ask if she wants to stay or go and she wants to go.

As we walk away, without prompting or having been discussed, our girl looks back. I didn't know what is coming next but what happens stops me in my tracks.

Madison, stops, blows her mom a kiss and said, 'Bye, Mom."

Madison is so much stronger than we gave her credit for. I don't know why I doubted her.

After all, she is her mother's daughter.

We have another tough day ahead.

I gave my final remarks to Hannah Friday before her cremation Saturday. I wish it was that easy to close the book. Instead, every place I look brings her back to mind.

Considering what we were doing, I felt Friday's trip to the funeral home to see the body went about as well as you could expect. Madison shocked us all – she really did make us all proud with how she handled it. Although I was pacing like a caged tiger, I was able to get through the experience without losing my grip. I prepared my daughter – and in turn myself – for what was coming, and we made it through to the end.

However, the things you don't prepare for can be crippling. Those sneaky moments that blindside.

After Madison's goodbye – that I had been stressing about pretty much constantly since I made the decision to do it – went well, I sort of let my guard down.

We go back to (Hannah's brother) Mike's place and I actually fix a small plate of food. This is practically the first food I have tried to eat since my world crumbled. I fix Madison a plate and sit her at the dining room table and then collect some small portions of a few items and sit down next to her.

I spoon the nearest spot on the plate and bring it to my mouth. As the casserole enters my mouth, I am in trouble. My throat narrows, my stomach churns, and I become nauseous.

Hannah has three brothers. The oldest is Ken. His fiancé Brenda made a hash brown casserole.

It was a sweet gesture as this is a dish Hannah was known for. She made it for us practically every holiday for the last twenty years. And it is my favorite.

As the combination of the smell, the taste, and texture mixes in my mouth, I have a physical reaction to it. Uncontrollable, without warning ... as my mind processes one more thing that has been ripped away.

I could care less about the casserole, no matter how much I always enjoy it. But the finality of it all sends my brain spiraling into iterations of the other smaller parts of our life that left with her. The casserole was a symbol of all that is lost - the depth of how different my life will be from this point.

The television series we binge-watched. Our favorite vacation spots. Those restaurants where we had great memories.

I prepared mentally to see the body and that went fine. I assume future birthdays and holidays will be similar. I am a planner. I have prepared to handle the visitation Sunday. But the surprises are whipping me.

She had a smile that could light up the sky. Occasionally, I would do something that invoked her smile - and make it radiate through her eyes. It was intoxicating to experience and I lived for those moments. Lately, they had occurred less and less. And that haunts me.

Like many I assume, our marriage wasn't where I wanted it to be when this happened. I was working a lot and as time progressed, we were more like close friends than star-crossed lovers.

Time and circumstances can dictate that I suppose, but it is hard to accept now that she is gone. Why didn't I address it? Why didn't we communicate better? Where were my priorities? I'm the one with all the word skills - I should have taken a day to myself and composed how deep down, I really only wanted to make her happy. Desperately.

As I lie awake at night, those questions just won't subside. So, this is what pain feels like? I only thought I knew before.

I have read this is all a process. That it will improve gradually but likely never go away. I am staying busy – Madison will make sure I do. She is a great kid and she doesn't deserve what she has been burdened with.

Today we will meet visitors as they pay their respects. I'm told there will be a big crowd - as Hannah was admired by many. I will see people from our shared past. We will hug, and cry and I won't even pretend to be OK.

What I really need today are smiles. And I know, they won't be like the one that stole my heart 25 years ago. But as you come up to me, Madison, and our devastated families, please do that for me. For us. For Hannah.

Seeing all those faces from our past are going to flood back memories that I fear will lead somewhere dark. Just for today Lord, please limit the "hash brown casserole" moments.

Just give us your best smile. And lend me some strength.

I think I miss her smile the most.

There are hundreds and hundreds trying their damnedest to substitute their smiles in her place. The visitation is loaded with love as mourners provide a steady stream for around two solid hours. The support is overwhelming. Unmistakable. My wife and her family touched a lot of lives and so many felt they have no choice but to pay their respects.

This isn't an easy thing to do ... to publicly say goodbye. To greet the emotionally destroyed family while you are still processing this tragedy yourself. Most of us have been on both sides of that visitation line. Neither side are lined with rainbows and lollipops.

Hundreds make their way into the small funeral home. Some had known Hannah her entire life. Others needed a GPS to find her small-town origins and then needed introductions to her family. But the crowd and many others who want to be there all wait patiently, one at a time, and pass through to offer whatever words they can muster to the family.

My focus heading into today has been to prepare Madison for the day. On the three hour drive up this morning, I explain how I expect the day to transpire. We will go to "Uncle Mike's" (Hannah's brother) and eat a bite before putting our dress and suit on. Madison's cousins Katlyn and Riley will help with her dress and makeup. Dad isn't quite up for that – and they will make it fun for her. Finally, we will go back

to the funeral home where we said goodbye to "Mom" on Friday.

But Mom won't be there. She is gone. Then lots of our friends will come and say really nice things about your mom. Because they know how special she was – just like you and I still do. And how much they will miss her. And are sad like we are.

She pauses to process.

And we start over again.

Celebrating the Life of

Hannah Puzak Etheridge
January 15, 1973 ~ August 30, 2017

Bumpers Funeral Home
Sunday, September 3, 2017
2:00 P.M. ~ 4:00 P.M.

I don't know if that is the right thing to do but I really do think it helped. As the somber line filed past, Madison is content. Katlyn sat with her a few feet away from the receiving line. That way she can be seen and spoken to and also notice some friendly faces. She popped up a few times and made the rounds – like a rock star in a room full of adoring fans.

She blows us away with how she handled today. Our girl.

At the close of the day, Hannah's mom and I tell Madi she had graduated from girl to woman today. She smiled. I hope she knows how proud we are of her.

Another thing blows me away and that is just how many people show up. We obviously need a larger venue. How in the hell did I underestimate how many people will attend? I'm sorry for that.

The line snakes around the inside of the building and people stack up outside. I wait at the front of the reception line, as images from her life surround us. People from every stage of her life are there along with people who know her mom or one of her brothers, or my mom or sister, and basically some who really only knew Hannah through someone else who loved her.

There are many familiar faces. People you lose touch with. People you care about but have just failed to connect. Maintaining a friendship can be hard. Many found their way to see us today.

With some, you step right back into where you were. You just know they are there for you. And those are the ones that cloud my vision and bring tears.

After the last of the line ended, I feel a little relief. Two hours of individual conversations are exhausting. No breaks. And the topic, oh so heavy. I tried mixing up my responses as I grew weary of repeating the same phrases. But that becomes a fool's errand as creativity gives way to repetition. I am tired and not very articulate. The words really don't matter that much anyway. There isn't a whole lot of comfort given or received. The value is in the presence. That you are not alone in this world-tilting experience.

One thing that has provided strength this week is the outpouring of support. As I said on my personal Facebook page, the building was packed with love. You couldn't mistake it.

It lifted me. I felt less burdened. I let my guard down for a little. And I needed that.

After the visitation ends, the family heads back for a meal. Madison and I came over a bit late after changing clothes and decompressing for a bit. As I absorb the scene, there are all these smiling faces enjoying their chance to reconnect. But someone is missing. She would have been right in the heart of the fun, flashing that beautiful smile that brought light to darkness.

And I had to walk away.

We pose for group photos. I thank everyone for being there for Hannah – I know it was hard for them to say goodbye to her. And we leave for home.

On the ride back, my mood lifts. It had been a good day – considering. Madison handled a gut-wrenching moment like a pro. You can't help but feel empowered by the show of support.

Madison started singing along with a song on the radio. I catch myself quietly joining in.

Oh My God, I had forgotten.

And like that, the guilt engulfs me. I start sobbing.

Madison notices and reaches over and pats my hand. Hannah used to do that. I cry harder.

I pull over to the side of the road.

"Daddy sad," Madison said. "Crying. Mommy gone".

Now it is her turn to help me.

I know it is OK to sing along with Madison. She needs that interaction. I know I shouldn't feel guilty for finding humor or a light moment. There's no tax for not being sad 24-x-7, regardless of the circumstances. Lord knows I've met that standard this week.

I get it together and we continue. An hour or so later, Madison started another vocal performance.

This time I belt it out with her – a duet for the ages.

And somewhere, we all know Hannah is smiling.

———————————————

The house sure is quiet.

Madison and I spent the night alone in our house after the visitation Sunday. I chose to do this – many have offered to intervene – because I want us both to see what the new situation is going to feel like.

Face it head-on. Rip the band-aid off. You can make anything sound good in your head.

We spent Monday together at the house. I went through our bedroom, boxed up some of Hannah's clothes, and just generally tried to organize. Our house was a wreck — because there had always been time to fix it later.

There always had been.

I don't understand why we are where we are. I know Hannah packed a lot of living into her 44 years. Still, there were so many things we always talked about but never got around to. We liked to travel. Over the years we went to Hawaii, Las Vegas, Nashville, Memphis, the Bahamas, Cozumel, The Cayman Islands, Orlando, and many others. We lived in Sumter County where we met but then also lived in Tuscaloosa, Marietta (GA), and Daphne two different times.

The one trip that stands out came when we visited New York City. This was her idea — kind of.

I had started running. Looking back, it was part of a mid-life thing, I suppose. But I liked how I felt afterward and got a lot leaner and healthier. I set a goal to run a half-marathon in Pensacola Beach and was able to do it. Hannah and Madison were there in the 30-degree temps to cheer me on. It was a good day.

After completing that goal, I was left searching for a "what's next?" I had watched a video on the New York City Marathon and flippantly remarked to her that if I was ever going to do a marathon, I would want to do one like that; with over a million people cheering you as you weave through all five NYC boroughs.

"You should do it," she said. "If you decide to do it, you will put in the training and you will do it. I know you. You are crazy enough that they will carry you off the course before you'll quit. Just go ahead and do it."

You can't just sign up for a race like that. You have to time-qualify (which wasn't physically possible for me) or be selected with long odds through a lottery. Besides, you need to be a little crazy to choose to run 26.2 miles without anyone forcing you.

She always supported me; even when it was something she didn't understand. To be honest, I failed to reciprocate with her in so many ways. Looking back, I sat in judgment of many of her ideas and only supported the ones I felt were worthy to me. I didn't meet her halfway and it took her death to recognize this. "Where did all these trees come from", he said from the forest?

On one hand, I feel like I have gained more clarity about our relationship in the past few days than in the years leading up to this. And on the other, I am so lost without her supporting whatever zaniness I push my body to this week.

I put my name in the NYC Marathon lottery – just as she instructed. We said if it was meant to be, I would be selected.

Somehow, I got in and I'll never forget what she said to me, "THIS would be the lottery you would win, now wouldn't it?"

I trained hard, but I didn't know what I was in for. During the race I injured my hip at mile 12. I knew she was waiting for me after I finished and there was no way I was disappointing her.

If only I had that mindset at other times through our relationship.

Her belief in me helped push through some very painful hours. She was right. I was going to finish what I started. And I did.

Now I am going to transfer her confidence in me to today.

I have often heard, "you don't have to be crazy to run a marathon. But it helps."

As I looked through some desk drawers, I found an old iPhone. After charging it, I found a video of Madison and Hannah singing an acapella version of Patsy Cline's, "Crazy". Y'all, I think I have watched it a hundred times.

I don't have to spell out the symbolism here. It writes itself.

There is no underestimating the challenge before us today. Each step presents a new obstacle, some I don't have much training for.

One thing I do know is that my wife demonstrated her belief in me consistently through our time together. I can't think it was a coincidence that in our first day in the house alone without her, this video of a moment long ago just appeared. And unlike so many other times where I didn't understand her methods, this time it came through crystal clear.

"I'm crazy for trying. Crazy for crying.

And I'm crazy for loving you."

Thanks babe. You always knew just what to say.

Author's Note: Here is a story I wrote for Hannah on her birthday a few years ago.

The first time I saw you was in the library. You were sitting there, pretending to study, and I knew from that point on the only studying I would do that day wouldn't involve a book.

An introduction, then a first date. You were so nervous you tore your burger into pieces. I couldn't believe someone like you was nervous being with me. I was hooked.

I learned about you; Your loving heart, your easy smile, your absence of ego. How you love animals, and ghosts, and seafood. And how you love Elvis because growing up when you heard his music on the way to school in the mornings, somehow it would always be a good day.

As the years moved on and you swapped Miss for Mrs., new challenges emerged. Job changes led to home changes, and then along came this sweet child locked away in a world inside her head.

Our life plan changed. Instead of little league or prom, we learned about IEPs and Special Olympics. While our friends were complaining about how their kids were back-talking them, we ached for a simple conversation with ours. Through all the dark times, the public meltdowns, her runaway phase, a house fire, her seizures, her body struggles, you faced them head on.

You have forsaken any expectation of privacy. You can't go to a public place without playing chaperone for multiple bathroom trips. You haven't sat through a full movie or restaurant meal in years. You can't have a relaxing day at home without worrying about someone cutting her hair or blowing up a microwave.

There are good times too. You've learned to appreciate moments many take for granted. An appropriate remark; a schedule change without a meltdown, or a night out with adult conversation.

Somehow you keep your wits about you during the dark times. Then when you find alone time to crash, you cry. And although sometimes we try, we know ours is a puzzle without all of the pieces.

Yeah, we are learning. And 25 years after that day in library, I'm still learning things about you.

I learned you are strong enough to handle anything except admitting to that strength. That you like a little coffee with your creamer, somehow need a jacket in August, and never feel you take a good photo. I've learned a girl can't ever have too many pairs of yoga pants, and if there are dirty dishes in the sink, it really isn't that big a deal. You make me laugh. You make me mad. And you make me want to make you proud.

Sure, life is hard sometimes. But our daughter didn't ask for these challenges any more than we did. And like her mom, she is resilient. Most days, she is a happy child. She doesn't have everything she wants but what she does have plenty of is love. And she knows her mom will always be there for her because you always have been. Somehow, whether we can believe it or not, next month she turns 18.

Time stands still for no one. Yet, somehow, you remain just as stunning as you were that day in library. Today is your birthday. And I'm honored you chose to spend this day, like so many others, standing by my side facing life together. I'm sure it will be a great day. Because, my dear wife, you deserve nothing less.

But just in case, here's a little Elvis to start the day.

I didn't sob today.

Isn't it something when you are laying prone on rock bottom, just how far away that first rung of the ladder appears?

In my adult life, I don't ever recall really sobbing. Crying, sure? Like when Clemson ran the pick play to beat Alabama last year. That was seriously sad.

But an uncontrollable sob that just grips your soul? I don't recall those. I had been so fortunate.

After Hannah's passing last Wednesday, I've just been hopelessly somber. I haven't been able to eat. I've lost close to 15 pounds. I can't sleep. I had nine hours total sleep in five nights. This is rock bottom.

Today was something above rock bottom.

We'll take it.

I spent time this week working on after-school options for Madison. We think we have it worked out where we have an option, one she will enjoy along with a good choice for me. Her teacher has been incredibly helpful – an above the call-of-duty effort – and each person we've come in contact with has been so supportive. Madison will also go to the Exceptional Foundation for after-school care. In fact, they started an after-school program using Madison as the catalyst for it. People continue to step forward.

Friends who haven't called or texted in years are checking on me regularly. I have reached out to some of Hannah's friends as well as I try to process where we go next.

A co-worker arranged for Madison to get a hair-styling Thursday. Madi has school pictures Wednesday and my mom was available to take her to the stylist. The hairdresser, Amelia (Studio 31 in Spanish Fort) was amazing. She made Madison feel so special on a week that was tough for all of us.

I got out of the house Thursday and visited a buddy. We talked about non-sad things – at least a little – and it helped. Just being away from the house for some time was important. Inside those walls, it seems there are ghosts everywhere we turn. I spent the night away from our house and actually slept a full six hours – the most since before my world slipped away with the six words, "we were unable to resuscitate her".

Tonight Madison, my friend John and I went out to eat. I was a bit worried about the new normal – like restaurants, movie theaters, ballgames, etc. because of Madison's frequent bathroom trips. Hannah always handled the obsessive, repetitive trips. It was a continued point of frustration for her.

And she could go in the ladies' room as a chaperon. How would I manage?

In case you were wondering, I am typically not allowed in the ladies' room. Some places have family bathrooms, but they are kind of rare. This is a part of the new reality that makes me uncomfortable. And while Madison is fully capable of going solo, she struggles with things like barging into occupied stalls, not closing the stall door, and other personal space type of fouls. I fear she will encounter someone not so understanding.

About ten minutes into our meal, Madison made the request. She apparently didn't want me to have to wait long – she is so considerate. We went, and I hovered outside in the corridor – getting strange looks as the creepy guy lurking.

I asked our server if she would mind checking on Madison and although she was busy, she happily obliged. Afterward, I explained the situation and she gave us hugs. We are seeing the best of people this week. And it is making me want to be a better person to earn these gestures.

After we ate, we walked around a sporting goods store. Madison wanted "workout clothes" so we looked around. We passed by a little outfit that just looked perfect for Hannah. I winced and put my arm around Madison as we walked.

"Sad," Madison said. It was if she knew exactly what I was thinking. Maybe she thought the same thing. Regardless, the daughter continues to help the father step through the darkness. Like her mother before her, Madison is providing strength.

Yes, I can still see rock bottom from here. But through the kindness of so many, I don't feel like a resident.

Thank you all.

We did it without you today.

One of the staples of our marriage has been college football Saturdays. All through the years, we have either cooked or bought a spread of food and just snacked and relaxed for much of the day.

Sometimes we had company over and other times it was just the three of us. We would discuss the menu all week and enjoyed looking forward to the food for the day almost as much as experiencing it.

Hannah was a good cook, but she really excelled at tailgate food. Her Buffalo chicken wing dip was legendary, but she did sausage balls, pigs-in-the-blankets and all kinds of other recipes she would find. We have some great memories of football Saturdays at home. Even during the strict diet in marathon training, I would enjoy all the decadence.

Hannah would often put on a cute, Alabama-themed outfit and even though she didn't care much for the other games, she would dial in for the Crimson Tide game.

Last weekend there was football but honestly, I couldn't watch. The wounds were too fresh. This week was easier, although still difficult. I went to a local restaurant and got some chicken fingers. On her first bite, Madison exclaimed, "delicious". She is trying her best to help her dad. She spilled her drink and instead of going into a meltdown as sometimes happens, she calmly said, "Sorry. Towel." That girl is keeping me sane.

There are so many activities that feel empty now. Hannah was such a big part of everything we did.

But today I made the effort. I ate. I had most of a beer. I engaged with Madison to encourage her to cheer during the game. It was by no means the same, but we at least made the effort. That is where we are right now – executing on tradition and routine as much as anything.

It was painful. But it was a step toward getting to our new normal.

Everyone says we need to get in a new routine. Forgive me if don't yearn a bit for my old one.

I started back to work today. It was necessary. People were nice – even if they do look at you differently than before. I assume those looks, like most things, will pass with time.

I have an hour commute to work and the morning trek was the worst part of my day. I turned the radio dial to anything and everything. I broke the law and checked Facebook as I drove. In the end, I ended up thinking about things I shouldn't think about. My mind is a place to avoid. Then a Luke Bryan song came on – "Drink A Beer". It is a song about losing someone and although I really didn't want to listen to it, I stayed until the end.

In some ways I feel I am courting misery.

In others, I feel I have accepted the new reality.

Madison is doing her best to help push me towards this scary new life. She is putting her shoes away. She helped me recline on the couch. She fixed her own drink refill. None of this was on my command. She knows way more than she lets on and she is showing she cares in her own way.

She also knows that if she keeps asking for blonde highlights, eventually Dad will cave. That day is coming – as the requests are mounting. Other than the hair fixation, she has been incredibly well-behaved since we said good-bye to Hannah's body at the funeral home. No real meltdowns. No teen-age attitude. Just trying to help anyway she can. Our girl.

She sent me a text today and told me, "I Love You". I didn't put her up to it. She did this completely on her own. If I didn't know better, I would think someone helped her. I continue to be floored by how she is providing me with support. I thought it was supposed to be the other way around. Yet, here we are.

A really nice lady (Misty) brought a home-made meal over for us today. She plans to do that every Monday during our transition. Everyone has been so supportive. I continue to struggle to understand how I earn this.

Madison greeted the meal with a "yum" and a "delicious". Sure, she liked it and ate most of it. But the vocal affirmations were for me. She knows that is what I want to hear. We are really growing closer in our grief.

As I ate the meal – and you know she was right as it was both "yum" and "delicious" - I couldn't help but feel a little guilty. I'm not sure why. We all have to eat after all. But the guilt was there and like an unwelcome house guest, tends to hang around a while once it arrives.

We are at the point now where there are few if any memories of Hannah that feel good. They are all painful. I understand at some point that may lessen, and if so, I'd like to get one of those giant countdown clocks if any of you have that date handy. I just want a break from sadness.

In the interim, we just persevere. We go to school, to work, and do household chores. We talk about coloring our hair and planning our week. Just like before, except there is a giant hole to avoid.

Yes, we are working on that routine everyone says we need. Meanwhile, Madison is helping her dad keep his sanity. And if he springs for blonde highlights along the way, so be it.

For the first time in over ten days, Madison mentioned her mom today. It was a slip. And her face looked like she had seen a monster.

I had asked her if she wanted to watch TV and if so, in what room? She answered, "bedroom". I asked her, "in your bedroom or in mine?"

Her mouth tumbled out, "Mommy's bedroom."

The look of horror on her face was heartbreaking as she quickly changed her answer to her own bedroom and scurried away.

I stood for a minute, contemplating her words and my move.

I watched her trot away alone into her room. I badly wanted to flee upstairs to my own room. In fact, I started that way. But I stopped.

I tracked her down and we sat on her bed and talked about her mom; how it is OK to talk about Mommy. That Mommy was a huge part of our lives for so long, that doesn't just stop because she isn't here. Mommy took care of us and she wanted us to be happy. We can talk about Mommy anytime we want. I want you to talk about Mommy anytime you want to. Madison listened.

In that scene, I felt a vibe like I was a sitcom dad who has all the answers. Of course, a few weeks ago I didn't seem to have any of them. I am drowning in perspective now and left wondering why it took losing my wife to reflect on shortcomings as a husband and father.

The other side of that is the person who would value most all of this "enlightenment" isn't here to see any of it. I'm left trying to project these husbandry failings in a role as father, son, brother, or friend. I feel cheated – and certainly feel Hannah was shorted as well. That is hard arithmetic to solve.

Wednesday made it two weeks from when our world shifted. In some ways it feels much longer ago than that. So much has changed. I recall the hopelessness of the first few days; the visits, the calls and texts. The general overwhelming urge to rage at the world, at God, at myself. Some of that has tempered with time. Some of it is bubbling under the lid – awaiting an opportunity to release.

I got angry today; irrationally angry. Hannah had purchased concert tickets for Madison back in May. Madison had it listed on her calendar and discussed it frequently. Last week, we briefly considered skipping it before realizing that Madison has lost so much, she needs to go to that concert.

After Hannah's passing, I called the ticket company to see how to access the tickets. Due to her death, they tried to cancel the tickets and I told them not to, that we still wanted to go. They said they would email the tickets to me.

I found out today why I had not received the tickets. They canceled them anyway, against my wishes. The concert is this Friday.

If you have ever been that parent defending your child, you probably know how that next dialogue went. In the end, they couldn't produce what they didn't have but they did all they could to make it right. Long story, short, we are still going to the concert.

But to quote a phrase from my grandmother, "I acted ugly".

Madison was there to listen and as I moved from room to room to avoid her, she just followed me. I was apparently good entertainment. It was the first time I had lost my temper – out loud anyway – in a long time.

Since Hannah's passing, our firsts are hard. The first night alone. The first morning school or work routine. The first trip to one of "our" restaurants. Now, the first temper tantrum. And coming Friday, the first trip to the cemetery. All tough.

Madison had a first tonight of her own as her mom's name slipped out. The look of terror on her face made me worry about how she is coping – she has been so on-level since the first few days. How much inner turmoil is she keeping hidden, so she doesn't upset me? There's one more thing to feel guilty about.

She had enjoyed a great day. It was picture day and our new favorite stylist Amelia surprised her at school and did her hair and makeup. Madison looked amazing.

All I can do now is channel "Sitcom Dad", maybe the one from Growing Pains. He always knew what to do. What he would likely say is to face this head on; to talk more to Madison about her mom so nothing is taboo. She needs to feel safe enough with you that if something slips out, that it is OK. This is all new for her too.

Now I think I'll head up and watch a little TV. Maybe Growing Pains is on. And you know what? I think I will watch it in "Mommy's bedroom."

Madison is sound asleep across from me. I lie awake, bouncing imaginary balls across the corners of the room.

We are in Livingston, at Hannah's brother Mike's place. We are in his guest bedroom – which Mike always called Hannah's room. But tonight, there is a vacancy.

In a few hours we will go out to the cemetery where Hannah's ashes are buried. I don't really know what to expect. Up to this point we have handled the big things, the viewing, the visitation, etc. without falling into a hole. It has been the things you don't prepare for that get you.

I knew making the trip to see Hannah's family without her could have some peril. She and her brother Mike were tight. He is taking this hard.

I appear to be farther along in my grief than Mike is. I think it may be because I saw Hannah every day. I have been forced to face it. Mike, he lives three hours away. You know, we could just be between visits. The hurt in his eyes cut through you. This is another reason I can't sleep, a reminder that the pain from this has fired indiscriminately hitting those close to her the hardest – but also affecting those watching from a distance.

I have moved out to the living room now. There's no use pretending I am going to sleep tonight, lying prone in Hannah's room. Maybe next trip. Another "first" checked off the list.

I am out in the living room, with lights on and a ceiling fan clicking to me. Against the wall there are photos from Hannah's visitation. I can't seem to look away. She is smiling in every photo and I remember the backstory to each one.

I so want to experience a happy memory of her. God knows, there were so many.

There is a photo of a zoo trip with a young Madi. Another of Special Olympics where the theme was mustaches and Hannah has a bad, fake mustache with a cheesy grin. There are a couple of Mardi Gras balls, her parents' fiftieth wedding anniversary, a family beach photo along with her in an Alabama football jersey.

I miss that girl.

And I am not alone.

A few people have asked me why I share so much publicly. I admit I was hesitant to start, putting your regrets and faults out there for people to sit in judgment. There is a vulnerability, a nakedness to it that I wasn't sure I was up for. Frankly, I still have my doubts this is the right thing to do.

However, at that point I was searching for answers and the process of organizing my thoughts forced that structure. I remember thinking there is nothing anyone could say to make me feel any worse than I do right now. So, if this helps my grieving process, then that's what we will do.

Instead, I have found tremendous value with the public feedback. Perhaps the best part is the reinforcement that we are not alone in this. People legitimately care. And it has forced me to interact more than I would have otherwise.

I am lonely. I lost twenty-five years of friendship where she was my first contact for happy, sad, mad, and of course, love. Feeling the support, hearing people tell me how they can relate, and that they are attempting to make changes in their own lives has boosted me.

Lemonade out of lemons. Or something like that.

We can't change what happened. We may never know any of the why's. All we can do is keep pushing ahead. Slow is OK. Sad is OK. Vulnerable is OK.

I am desperate for that happy memory. I have faith it will come.

And that will become a new happy memory all of its own.

We screamed. We sang. We danced.

It was just what we needed.

Friday had been a hard day. We visited Hannah's family without her. That was difficult. We visited the graveside for the first time since her ashes were set. And then we attended the concert that Hannah had planned for us all months ago.

Madison had been doing so well but today was tough for her. Surrounded by photos that triggered memories of her mom along with situations where Hannah was her lifeline, we had a bit of an episode today.

Frankly, this is what we had been expecting long before now.

She and I were sitting cross-legged at the foot of Hannah's grave. Ants scurried over my leg as I talked out loud to my late wife. Madison was engaged. So much so that she began repeating each word as I spoke.

Talk about pressure to choose the right words ... not only did I need to make sense in what I said to Hannah, but I needed to use words that Madison understood. Fortunately, Hannah seemed to play along. We played this repeat game for about five minutes, a long time to stay on-point within a limited vocabulary range.

I think Madison really wanted to talk to Hannah. She just didn't have the words. So, she did the next best thing and borrowed mine. If only I had been more articulate.

After we wrapped up, we went back to Hannah's brother Mike's place to get ready for the concert. As we killed time, she started to focus more on the photo collages. I totally get it, they had mesmerized me the night before. In a few minutes she started to mention the word sad ... followed by heartbroken. This is what we had been discussing when Hannah had come up previously. That was obviously where her mind was.

A few minutes later the tears came, followed by the words, "Scooby Doo", "Shrek and Donkey", and "SpongeBob". These were all memories from our trip to Orlando back in May, and there was a photo in the collage from that trip. She was reliving that memory. And it made her sad.

And heartbroken.

We knew this was coming. Madison had repressed much of those feelings – she hasn't cried for Hannah since the early stages. She was really moody the remainder of the afternoon. But our girl worked her way through it.

But Friday was really two days. There was the sad one. Then there was the one that began with a scanned ticket into the Tuscaloosa Amphitheater.

We laughed. We smiled. We danced like no one was watching. We sang loudly, off-key, and messed up the words. It was glorious.

There were five of us together. Mike was with us as were two of Hannah's longtime friends, Christie and Beverly. Madison was insulated between all of us, surrounded by love and support – and she really enjoyed the night.

Over the years, Hannah had introduced Madison to concerts. I really wasn't part of that scene. I don't know why it ended up the way it did. This is yet another item Hannah loved that I failed to embrace. I had agreed to go to this one and was trying to make an effort to integrate into their concert bond. Unfortunately, I made the move too late and Hannah wasn't around to see it.

Madison was missing her role model, so she watched the rest of us, some girls in front of us, and mimicked much of what we did. She rocked, she swayed, and she did the cutest little hand gesture dances.

I can't remember when I have enjoyed a concert more. Hannah would have had a blast watching Madison and I frolic playfully. She would have complained when we wanted to sit down. She would have wondered if we could get down closer to the stage. She would have been hoarse before the main act took the stage. She would have done it her way.

Tonight, we did Hannah's thing – concerts – but we did it our own way. I sense that will be a familiar tenet as we head into this new reality.

Madison was watching me closely. Without Hannah there, she drank from her water bottle each time I did. She clapped when I clapped and sang when I sang.

Just like earlier in the day when we talked to her mother, we worked together to enjoy the concert. And we did enjoy it.

We had been looking for a break from sad and here it was, arriving on the heels of a rough afternoon. I had been a tad fearful the concert would be another somber nod to Hannah. Instead, we made it a celebration, an oasis that wasn't a mirage.

We missed you Babe. We may not have done it exactly like you would have but made it our own. Somewhere, somehow, I can't help but feel there was one more singing and dancing along with us.

I went for a run today.

It was needed. Overdue, even.

Through the past few years, running has been my stress relief from work concerns, problems with Madison and the occasional argument with Hannah.

Hannah would often joke if on a day where I was a little reluctant to go for a run that she could start an argument to get me going. I was a good runner mad. Like most long-time couples, she knew which buttons to push.

I wish she was here to start one with me now.

She never shared my interest in running. She ran with some girls occasionally. She ran with me once.

Once.

It was, honestly, one of the best runs of my life. I did nothing but compliment her and afterward I pleaded for a sequel.

She wasn't interested. I think she felt a little patronized because we were at different levels. I didn't care about that. I only was interested in her companionship, of sharing something that was important to me with her.

I have had a lot of guilt about not meeting her halfway on some of her interests. She would probably say the same if the roles were reversed.

Her last text to me was to tell me about a 5K where experienced runners like me run pushing special needs children in wheel chairs. She knew I would enjoy doing that for someone, trying to make it fun for them, and was pointing out an opportunity. She commented we could get Madison involved as well.

The night she passed, there was no chance of sleeping. My dad and stepmom were at the house, so Madison was covered in case she awakened. Sometime around midnight, I went for a run.

No music, no gadgets. Just a man and his mourning.

I didn't make it around the block when Tropical Storm Harvey's first lightning bolt greeted me. Wind howled. A hard rain followed. I remember realizing that I should probably go back. But I kept moving. I was running mad.

Why was she gone? What do I do now? How would Madison ever make it a week without Hannah, much less forever? For someone with such little feet, she left big shoes to fill. I was overwhelmed.

Alone, angry, confused; this was a memorable trip around the neighborhood. Five miles later, clothes-soaked head to toe, I returned home.

I am not a particularly accomplished runner, but the long distances have forced me to learn how to deal with being uncomfortable. They call it being comfortable being uncomfortable. And perhaps all of that has prepared me for today. There is certainly a lot of uncomfortable. Of unpleasant. Of doing the hard thing when you'd rather lie in bed.

But I'm not sure there is much that can prepare anyone for this. I'm searching to find what works for me. Writing seems cathartic. I feel a little better after I run. I am getting more comfortable being uncomfortable.

I will keep running. It helps to reflect, to wrangle the tangle inside my head. I still don't have many answers. But I have a little more peace. Today is better than yesterday.

Step by step, minute by minute, mile by mile; just keep moving forward.

I heard it well before I saw it. Before I knew what had happened, I was on the shoulder of the road.

The mind can be a funny thing.

After a minute or so, the ambulance went speeding by me. I had not only maneuvered to give it a wide berth, in my haste I almost wrecked in the process.

The siren triggered something inside me and before I realized what I was doing, I was imagining a scene I didn't even witness.

Inside the ambulance lay a wife and mother fighting for her life. Paramedics were using a defibrillator as they tried to keep her alive. And all I can do is nothing at all.

I got out of the way for this ambulance today early and with room to spare.

I never saw Hannah in her ambulance. I was at work an hour away. I didn't get to say goodbye or even know how serious her condition was. All I knew was she had fainted and was being taken by ambulance to the hospital.

I have a lot of questions about that day when her heart stopped at 15:32 and mine skipped a beat a few minutes later.

That phone call I received from Hannah's phone by a co-worker. The brief conversation I had with Hannah after she passed out but before she coded for the first time. Did she hear my final words before the phone went silent?

Those three little words that took forever to say to her when we started dating but she heard until she was tired of them throughout the marriage. Please tell me those last three words I said to her where the last three she heard.

She knew. But I'd like to think she received that reinforcement in her time of distress. She had to be afraid. And I was an hour away thinking all she had done was fainted.

Since her passing, some items strike me differently than before. That is only natural. Context changes most things. An ambulance siren; a funeral procession; the smell of coconut oil; cupcakes and frou-frou coffee; Spanish moss. They all remind me of her for different reasons.

Today, before I was aware of my actions, I was driving 70 on the shoulder of the road. The ambulance rolled by and I righted my path. In comparison, a car's path is easy to correct.

The thing with the ambulance kind of surprised me. I had not previously focused on that part of her passing. But when I heard the siren, it prompted something that had been lurking. I not only pulled over but was unhappy with those who took their time to make a lane.

One of the interesting aspects of the last three weeks has been how we are affected differently by stimulus. I am beginning to handle Hannah's loss a little better. This week has been easier than last week. But the nice gestures, the Samaritans bringing meals over; the strangers sending gifts and well wishes; the friends I haven't talked to since I was a boy reaching out to lend support; the special accommodations made for Madison — all of those are still buckling my lower lip.

Everyone handles these situations differently. Sometimes, like the example today, you don't even know how you will react until prompted. There undoubtedly will be other catalysts unearthed in the coming months. Some will probably come out of nowhere like the siren surprised me today.

I just hope eventually that surprise will emerge and trigger something positive. To remind me of a time when those three little words were not only heard but volleyed back.

Those words were the last I said to her. Yes, the call may have ended early, but she went out knowing she was loved.

I still hope she heard them one final time.

They are over 2,000 strong and they all have their whole adult lives in front of them.

It is a career fair at Auburn and my company is hiring. As face after face walks by, it is hard not to think back to my own time in college. That time before the real world started.

I met Hannah in February of my freshman year of college. That was so long ago it seems like it was someone else. She was a high school senior studying in the University library. I found studying in my room wrought with temptations. As it turns out, the library had a temptation of its own with blonde hair, green eyes, and a soft spot for a (then) gangly, country boy.

Back then we were going to go places and do things. I suppose we did, although the reality didn't match the visions from way back when.

We had caviar dreams and potted meat means. There is nothing wrong with potted meat, mind you. Add in a cracker on the river bank and you've got a nice Saturday. But despite the many things we did accomplish, it never seemed to match what those wide-eyed kids had envisioned.

In those days we were going to make a fortune, have a big family and grow old together. None of those actually materialized despite hard work and a few breaks along the way. Now here I sit far from poverty but not collecting beach condos like monopoly pieces either. Me and Madison are a family of two. Hannah left me a widower after 22 years of marriage. That hurts to type.

There's a magnet pulling me towards disillusionment. I'm resisting but the draw is there.

I always assumed Hannah and I would celebrate a fifty or maybe even sixty-year wedding anniversary. Other times I wondered if we would make it through until tomorrow. That's real life after all. The hard times come. If you are lucky, they also depart. I couldn't imagine she would vanish so quickly. It seems like we just got started a few moments ago.

We are now at three weeks out, I am starting to see some sunshine peeking out of the clouds. Food has taste again. I've expanded the sleep pattern to four hours a night. Talking about it helps. Family and friends have stepped forward to help me try to make sense of the new normal, especially all of these firsts. But there are so many remaining to experience.

In a way, the career fair was a nice change. It was a chance to impart some of this hard-earned wisdom to another generation. They undoubtedly have some of the big dreams that Hannah and I had back in the mid-1990's. And while I am not qualified to tell them how to achieve them, I can certainly understand where they are coming from and provide a nudge in the right direction.

The students today in many ways are more advanced than we were back in our day. Technology has brought the world closer together. We now know everything as it happens. No one has time for patience or for dreams to materialize organically. Dreams are important. But perhaps what is more important is hope. Both were dashed in an ER family room three weeks ago. But they can return. They have to return. No, they won't be the same as before. That 22-year-old me really didn't understand life anyway. He focused on material things. People are now of greater importance.

We can't go back. We can't change a thing. All we can do is somehow build new dreams. And sprinkle in a little hope to go with it.

I had a good day Thursday.

I caught myself smiling. I noticed birds. I was myself for a little while. Maybe even a little better than that.

Last night, I checked my phone for text messages.

"I have had a bad couple of days," one said.

Another followed, "I miss her so much. How are you?"

And just like that, it was gone.

I couldn't answer those with, "for the first time in three weeks, I didn't feel a tear roll down my cheek".

Because why today? I'll likely start a new streak the next day. But on this one day, yesterday, it was tolerable. Even better than that.

I am in the foxhole. I am living her loss 24x7. There have been few breaks, few opportunities of respite. I am coping, sometimes not so well. But yesterday I felt better.

But I didn't even want to admit that to anyone. I know no one expects me to be sad every minute of every day. Sometimes, I do feel that is the expectation.

I got a prescription to help me sleep. The second night with it I slept nearly six hours. That almost matched the first week total. I am still up before four, but I'll just use the time to write, to help brush out the tangle in my mind. And I do feel a little better, even at the sleep deficit. Gradual progress, they say.

Yesterday I woke up in a good mood. I got Madi ready for school. She was grouchy, and it looked like a meltdown was imminent. But we worked through it. By the time the bus came, she was her normal happy self. I did that, with her help. Each little victory empowers us both.

I called a friend on the way to work. It filled that alone commute time so well. We laughed, we shared, we just were. I needed it.

Work was busy. There were many meetings. I got to make some decisions. I got to jump into the middle of a squabble. I was ready for all of it, surprisingly enough.

But there is a fine line. I'm a memory away from falling off that high wire.

I talked to a coworker who lost her daughter nearly twenty years ago. Her pain is still deep. And I don't understand how that translates to my situation. I don't want to hurt forever. But is that what I am facing?

So few answers.

I called another friend on the commute home. That is my worst time because I used to talk to Hannah then. We would download our days to each other. Funny how I miss our phone talks as much then as I do the ones in person. Talking to the friend helped. The people in my life are rewarding me for my taste in friends.

When we arrived home, Madi had a package in the mail. Inside it was a necklace with a photo of her mom on one side and an inscription, "In Loving Memory Hannah Etheridge" on the other. She smiled when she saw it. She calls it her "Hannah necklace", because of the inscription. We are literal with labels.

This is a another incredibly sweet gesture in what is becoming a long line of generosity. It follows the prior day's surprise from the Exceptional Foundation where the adults in that program – Madison's new peers from her after school program – all made her cards. There were the simplest, but sweetest messages you will ever see. And they sent her gift cards. That girl of ours can charm you without saying a word. I am so proud of her.

People are reaching out. I am trying to accept help. Honestly, that is just one more new skill I am having to develop. I am self-reliant. But I have learned about limits.

Who knows what the next day brings?

I hope for another good day. I want to hear birds singing and notice leaves turning color. I want to smile and not know why. I long for an easy day.

It wasn't easy by any means, but it was a good day, a better day. And hopefully soon there will be another one.

"She's gone."

Madison was having a rough morning. She had a big breakfast. She had her favorite show on television. She had her I-pad beside her and her drawing pad was in front of her.

The things that usually serve as fit busters were not working.

Then she said the word I felt was coming but hoped would not.

"Heartbroken."

That makes two of us.

She has coped amazingly well. But we all have our bad days. Weekends are a problem for both of us.

I told her I was sorry. That I wish I could fix it. I know she misses "Mommy".

"She's gone," Madison said.

And we were worried she wouldn't understand. She didn't cry as the words emerged. Her delivery was matter of fact. Just like, "Watch SpongeBob" or "Take a bath". But the delivery masked the inner turmoil.

She is grieving like the rest of us.

"Gonna be OK," she tells me; almost certainly parroting what someone had told her.

She is looking after her dad, protecting him. Hey, someone has to, right? Because Mommy's gone.

So, in her mind the job falls to her. Funny how the brain works, even one as complex as hers.

We talked through it. I don't know if it helped her. She's drawing now. There is a lady with blonde hair. Wonder who that could be?

Outwardly, Madison is doing great. She is embracing the independence. But inside she is facing the loss of her mother. And she can't talk about it the way we would. She did try a bit at the cemetery last week. She tried again this morning. I hope I am giving her what she needs, pushing the issue when I feel she is thinking of her mom. Like all of us, it will take time to work through it.

She understands. Sometimes I wish she didn't. That she had hope her mother would walk into the room at any time, smiling with hugs for everyone.

Instead, she understands. Her mother is gone. And she is hurting like the rest of us.

Another night passes and the sandman skips my bedroom.

The Ambien must be a placebo. The brain just won't shut off.

I am supposed to take Madison to the beach tomorrow. She is expecting it. She wrote it on her calendar. That means it happens. We'll push through and do that. Because fun is what she needs. And we have to get out of this damn house.

Like last night, my bedroom ceiling apparently needed supervising. It has been well-watched. Sleep has rarely been a problem for me through the years. These days it is rationed like water in the desert.

I don't understand it really. I should be a zombie. I should be sluggish. I should be making mistakes.

Instead, I am laser-focused. I am making good decisions. I am still able to form coherent thoughts, even on challenging subjects. The body has an amazing ability to persevere through trauma. I have been operating this way since August 30 at 3:32 PM. I'm sure this has a cost. Everything does. At this point I don't have a choice but to pay it.

So, I worry. You can imagine the topics. There's so much time trapped inside my head. There is no off switch, or even a pause. And that kind of scares me. This still feels new, even weeks in.

It is 1:49 AM Sunday morning. The cool crowd are probably closing down the bars. The married folks are sleeping near their spouse. For the first time in my adult life, I'm neither. And I don't understand what this other group I just received membership to is supposed to be doing.

I'm grieving Hannah as a person. I'm grieving our relationship. I'm grieving my daughter's mother. I'm grieving for the loss my family and friends also suffered. I'm over-grieved.

Earlier this week, I had a good day. Frankly, this weekend isn't going so well. I've been told that is part of the natural process. That if I didn't experience the lows, then there would be cause to worry. So, we just persevere and learn how to cope.

There is a new life to begin. I understand that. Madison has provided glimpses into her capabilities that enlighten us. It provides hope. She has so much to give. I will help her unleash it.

I feel I am doing a good job as her father, considering. We are growing close. Necessity forces the issue. I need that validation that something amid all this chaos is going well.

I miss my wife. I miss having someone to make witty remarks to. And having someone lob the banter back at me. We made each other laugh. Humor is how I coped with a lot of issues over the years and her passing robbed that from me as well.

I understand this is dark. But it is honest. Someday I will re-read this and remember. I hope there will be something to gain from it. To take stock of where my life is that point and use tonight as a comparison. I hope something positive comes out of this.

Until that time, I will reach out to friends and family. I want to try to earn all of the generous support we continue to receive. To be better than before. To not be the sad guy who can't sleep. So, there will be fun and frolicking. There will be humor. And Madi's calendar says there will be a beach trip. On Sunday.

The mud between her toes squished like walking on marshmallows. For someone with sensory issues, I wondered how Madison would respond.

"Like it," she said, as if she was anticipating my question. She seems to be doing that a lot these days.

Moments earlier she had bounded off the pier. The water was only four feet deep, but she still went under in a jumbled heap. I'm still standing on the pier wondering if I need to follow her in or give her a moment?

That's a question I keep asking myself these days ... how will she ever learn to be self-reliant if I am always hovering? So, I give her a few seconds. She rights herself with a big smile.

Madison enjoyed her swim. Afterwards we laid on towels on the pier. I would catch her watching me.

Without her mom, she has started copying a lot of what I do. I put on sunglasses, she finds a pair. I take a drink, she does as well. I never noticed this before, even with her copying Hannah.

This morning I slept in for a few minutes. Yep, I had about six, one-hour naps last night. Fist bump.

My mom was here to help get Madison ready. But instead of school, they are going to a doctor's appointment. The change in the routine bothered Madison and she had a bit of a meltdown. At one point, she exclaimed, "Moooooommmmm." That is a first.

We did the best we could but there is no way to provide her what she needs. Her mom is gone. She knows and understands but there is still the tendency to want to scream out. I get it. We all have our ways to cope. Her way is just as good as yours or mine.

She and I bought groceries the other morning. We were standing in the checkout line and looked over and saw some gum. I saw spearmint.

Hannah hated spearmint. That is not hyperbole. She absolutely hated it. She claimed the smell made her nauseous. She wouldn't kiss me if I had any. So, you know me, I made it into a thing.

I would keep a pack handy and surprise her with it on her car-seat. Once I worked it out to have a waiter bring her a plate with nothing on it but a stick of spearmint. One time she cooked a new dish and my only reply was, "I can barely even taste the spearmint."

To be honest, I don't really even like spearmint. But it was fun. We had a good time with each other. She got my humor.

As I stood in the grocery line, I saw the jumbo pack of spearmint gum. I smiled hard, my eyes got wet, and I couldn't snatch it up fast enough.

I'm chewing a piece now. No one is here to complain, no one to kiss. But I think Hannah would appreciate the joke.

Five guys sat at a table. No, not the burger chain. Five males sat at a table. A gentle breeze wafted in off the water on the back deck as a singer crooned a few feet away. Flamed oyster aroma penetrated the nostrils which in turn watered the palate. Drinks were cold and abundant.

The water bristled in the moonlight. A school of fish huddled up below the boardwalk waiting for someone to feed them. A bay boat puttered by. It was like a backdrop to a movie.

That is appropriate since it feels like I have been playing a character these past few weeks.

Over the last month I keep wanting to pull my phone out and send her a text. This has been one of the bigger adjustments.

When something cool happens, I reach. When something bad happens, again, my brain is conditioned for that response. When I see a concert that she would be interested in, now I just swallow hard, phone in hand.

Wednesday makes it four weeks since Hannah's passing. In some ways I have moved on. I have done things this month that she always did for us previously. That list keeps growing. I feel like I am pretending at times.

I never expected to need to be good at any of these things. In the past, I only needed to get by for a few days until Hannah could take back over. Lord forbid I become (just a little) domestic.

Surprisingly, necessity is the genesis of mastery. I'm better at preempting Madi's meltdowns and I was already pretty good at it. I'm paying closer attention because I have to. Like so many other items, the hyper-focus of the past month has provided skills that Hannah would have loved to see me display more often. Isn't hindsight perfect? I only hope that leads to wisdom and better results going forward.

Through this process, I have mostly moved out of the guilt stage. The first couple of weeks – and you can go back and read it – I was beating myself up for the missed opportunities in our relationship. There is still some of that but for the most part it has passed. Hopefully the lessons learned outlast the second-guessing.

Those smiles I was chasing have slid a generation. They are still a tremendous motivator but instead of mother they are now about daughter.

Now the current stage is more about learning how to be a single dad for Madison. This phase is definitely more constructive than the prior one. We are learning together what our roles will now be.

What are our new routines? How about this doctor visit? Who do we need to talk to get help with this issue? How does this fitted bra work again?

It is all a process. Madison and I feel the support everyone around us provides. People have been so complimentary and generous.

Tonight, brought another first as I got a night out with the boys. My mom watched Madison tonight, so I could search for some adult conversation. Or at least conversations with adults – I'm not sure how mature these guys are.

It was nice to get out and relax a bit. I did talk about Hannah some, but I tried to work into the conversation. It didn't dominate. And we hit a wide variety of topics, some of them were even true.

I somehow avoided trying to text Hannah. That was not insignificant. I'll take my victories where I can find them. Everyone was patient and kind. They even laughed at my forced jokes. Usually I am funny. Tonight, I felt like I was finding my way a bit, which at this point seems to be my assigned seat.

We talked about new beginnings. About life after you think your world ended but it didn't really. There doesn't have to be tragedy to teach lessons, although they certainly seem more apt to stick. We talked about how priorities shift. How something that used to feel important can be relegated to afterthought. We talked heavy, we talked light. We just talked.

Five guys sat at a table. At least one is searching for his path. But he isn't searching alone.

The movie backdrop moves on. The character heads forward to the next scene.

It is the scene of countless gossip sessions, hair-stylings and mirror selfies.

There have been so many firsts this month. I just had one which I didn't anticipate. Y'all, I just made my first trip to the ladies' room.

No, I'm not identifying differently or going through a gender transition. Nothing of the sort. But I'm now a single dad of a daughter and public restroom trips can be a bit of an issue.

We were driving on the interstate last night. We were in the midst of a long haul and it was time for a break. I pulled into a rest area hoping for my new traveling best friend, a family restroom.

We struck out. Just the traditional setup was there. I confirmed with the attendant.

Then he said, "Do you need to go in with her? I can close it."

People continue to step forward to help us. Strangers and casual acquaintances have joined our cult of assistance as Madison and I navigate life without her mother and my wife.

I accepted the offer. And I walked into my first ladies' room.

First off, the chandeliers were gorgeous. The Persian rugs, I believe these were from the Timurid Empire, were immaculate. There were cabinets stacked with potpourri that is reminiscent of The Rose Parade. I couldn't find a urinal – they must have been hidden behind the giant wall of mirrors. All of the towels were decorative. Hands magically dried themselves while simultaneously nail polish was applied. I went with "glitter sparkle", by the way.

Guys, I think we have been getting short-changed.

I may finally know why girls go in groups to the restroom? They need someone to share the experience with … like a trip to Disney or a Black Friday sale.

So many firsts. This one went great. So much so that I can't wait to try out the women's book club.

Author's note – this seems like a good time to interject a story from before Hannah's death. Six weeks prior to her passing, Hannah lost her father. This ended up being instrumental in how Madison coped with losing her mother. I wrote this piece about it at the time, ignorant to how this event would impact our daughter.

They sit against the wall in the hospital's family counseling room. This is one of those conversations you know are necessary. You want the answers, but then again you don't.

Four siblings look on, their mother seated in front at a table. They discuss the fate of the man down the hall in room 122. The nurse describes how it got to this point, their options for the coming days and setting expectations. These are hard conversations.

They hear the words no one ever wants to hear about a loved one.

"This is not a recovery situation."

They handle it as well as anyone can expect, considering the impending loss of a father, a husband. The message isn't necessarily a surprise but hearing those words spoken aloud, they do carry more weight.

The family is all in the same place for one of the first non-holidays in a long time. They would all be back together a week later as their wait, and his, ends.

Death is rarely a welcome visitor. But everyone seems ready, in no small part because the man facing the great unknown was.

In moments like these, we wish we had great words to share. Instead, most of us struggle. When it comes to choosing the right communication, we typically feel as useless as a salad fork at Dreamland.

Words bring little comfort. Even the best-turned phrases fall hallow.

Most of us don't know what to say. We want to come up with something comforting or memorable to aid our loved ones through their sorrow. Instead, we typically just fall over our words in between embraces and "thoughts and prayers" mentions.

There's no playbook. Everyone needs something different. Sometimes it is answers. Other times it is a shoulder to lean on. Some want to return to their routine as soon as possible. At times it is just to be left alone.

The rest of us, we want to help, to do something. We bring food, or flowers, or cheer. We tell stories, we hug necks and we try to do it with a stiff lower jaw.

The best person I know in these situations is my grandmother. At 91, she has seen her share of loss. I have seen her walk into a room, identify a person hurting and with only a few sentences coax an unlikely smile; somehow create an island of respite in a sea of anguish. Hers is a gift few of us have. I asked if she had any tricks to share in these moments.

"Just hug them up and tell them you love them," she said. "They know you love them but that is about all you can do. It is a sad time. There is really nothing more you can do. When (her husband) died, I talked about picturing him with (his) ma and pa, his brothers and sisters and going fishing with his buddies. Just remember, he is in a better place than we all are."

And then without breaking breath, "I wish I could cook them something."

I know. Me too. I've got food on the grill. I don't know what else to do.

She had been smiling just minutes earlier.

Then came the clues. "Sad," said under her breath.

"Gone," and of course that clicked.

Madison is thinking of her mom. We spent the prior few minutes in a park feeding ducks and fish. I had just been thinking Hannah would have enjoyed the morning. I guess the apple doesn't fall far from whatever it is I am supposed to be.

I hoped to head off the potential sadness by heading over to get lunch. We are with friends, and our hosts had all these great options for us. As we sat down at the table, the meltdown started.

No matter how many times you endure it, the feeling is always the same. Helpless.

Like many people, I like to control situations whenever I can. This is one where there isn't much you can do. You still try. You coax. You distract. You plead.

I don't get embarrassed by them anymore. I admit I used to. I felt like every eye in the place was staring in judgment. These days that doesn't affect me the same way. Get your eyeful. I just feel bad for Madison.

Once she gets to that point, it really is too late to flip the channel. So, we go outside. We try to give her food. But this meltdown wasn't about food. We couldn't mitigate this one. There's no new heart to exchange for a broken one.

So, we try to distract. We walk back to the vehicle.
We talk about different activities, different food
options. Eventually we find one she is sort of excited
about. Love that chicken from Popeyes.

"Popcorn chicken," she said. I didn't know there was
such a thing. But when we see the menu there is
thankfully a popcorn chicken just as she said.

The meltdown ends.

After the meal, we leave our hosts for the long drive
home. Both of us have too much time to think. We
try to talk. I ask her about being sad. I ask her about
her mom. She doesn't volunteer much; just echoes
back my own questions that I end up answering.

I tell her I am sorry she feels like screaming. I tell her
that I had screamed on the commute to work one
day. I haven't told anyone else that.

That morning I just kept thinking things I shouldn't
and at that point I couldn't take it anymore. The
emotion came out with volume. I really didn't feel
any better about it afterward. But it came out just
the same.

She listens. I don't know what she understands.

It turns out, Madison had been thinking about her earlier episode. She starts to cry a bit. Then she tells me, "Sorry, screaming."

That is a first.

She has endured hundreds of meltdowns, many worse than the one Sunday. She has never verbalized any of it after the fact.

I know she is looking after me. She wants to help. She wants to make this impossibly hard situation easier for both of us.

"Helper", she says as we pull into the driveway. She grabs her suitcase and lugs it into the house. This is a new endeavor for her. She is helping.

A little while earlier, I had been trying to help her. Now it was her turn to return the favor. She's done more than that, though. She's given me a reason to keep pushing through tears, screams and that weight sitting on my chest.

One day, we will go back and feed ducks again. We will continue to do things that remind us of her mom. We will get through it.

Me and my helper.

———————————————

There were so many things we planned to do.

Places to go. People to see. Life to live.

Hannah ran out of time as did my life with her.

I have been thinking about that quite a bit lately. How there are a laundry list of experiences we always wanted to do but somehow never made them happen.

She did do a lot of things she wanted to do. Some she did without me. In hindsight, I guess that was best for her.

But when we pass on, all of those Earthly experiences stop. For many of us, when that time comes there will be so much we still want to do.

This is a topic I have talked about with several people since she passed. People of different ages, different roles, different outlooks. The one common tenet between them on those missed opportunities, "we felt we would get to it eventually."

A funny thing happens as we age. That experience you were really interested in at thirty isn't always as appealing at fifty. So even if you can check it off the list, the experience isn't what it could have been.

WHEN you do it can be almost as important as THAT you do it.

There were experiences I wanted to have with Hannah. She had similar wishes as well. We got to do some, but for others there was always a responsibility or an obstacle in the way.

Some obstacles were financial but not every interesting experience is expensive. I thought about that over the weekend as we visited places on a college football Saturday. For much of my married life, I worked hard through the week and basically claimed Fall Saturdays as my time. Did I really need the whole day? What I wouldn't give to have a Saturday back now to do something she would enjoy. Perspective comes along like a kidney stone on your wedding day. Again, timing is everything.

Ironically, I basically missed the month of September. I couldn't tell you what happened in the world. If I didn't live in Alabama where you can't avoid it, I'm not sure I would even know who has been winning those games I used to feel I couldn't miss.

Much of that time I spent taking stock of my life. What I liked. What I need to do better. What I would fix if I could. And where do we go from here? It still bothers me I never did that before.

I don't know how Hannah would feel about all this introspection? I feel she underestimated how people cared for her. She was complicated, and I never really figured her out. That might have been part of the allure, that puzzle to slot together when you feel there just might be a couple of pieces missing. I like interesting people. I liked her. I loved her. Those two are not always aligned.

She left us prematurely. We can't do anything about it. We just learn, we process, we grow. We make new plans.

And we attack them with a sense of urgency.

There are so many things I plan to do. Present tense.

And as we have learned the hard way, yes, timing matters.

There isn't much else I know to do.

Madison is crying again. She cries at school. She cries during her after-school program.

Of course, she cries at home, surrounded by memories of her mom.

It was her mom's house. We just lived here. Every room, every picture, every blemish has a story. And Madison can't seem to turn them off. I'm not the one to give advice on how to do that either.

It took her about a month. We had marveled at how well she was holding up. She did amazing. She was focused on helping her dad.

One of the first conversations we had after Hannah's passing was how I would help her, and she had to help me. She took that to heart and really has tried to assist however she could.

But the finality of our new reality seemed to pounce on her in the last week. She is just inconsolable. She has cried more this week than at any time after that first day.

Activities she used to enjoy, she ignores. People she used to light up and greet, she just stares blankly at them. Foods she would devour, she now just picks at.

This has been going on for a few days now. I am struggling with it. I can't fix it. All I can do is try to console her. Words are little help. I just want to hug the hurt away; a nice thought but futile as a strategy.

This week I have tried to hang with her each evening as she cried. I talked to her. I hugged her. I cried with her. I don't know if it helped her. It certainly didn't help me any. Frankly, her delayed reaction has been a setback for me.

Tonight, I tried something different. After she cried a bit, I saw her looking at me. I felt maybe she was keying off my sadness, my response. So, I got up. I left her crying. I folded laundry. I listened from just outside the room. In a few minutes, she stopped crying. She started talking about hair.

She started playing music on her I-Pad. I came back in the room smiling. Happy thoughts, happy mood. I was a big faker.

We are both sad. So often since August 30, I have felt like I was playing a character. I am definitely in full DeNiro mode now. I am pretending I am not sad. I am pretending to have answers for her. And we'll try this for a while, since wallowing in our misery wasn't doing either of us any good. And when this doesn't work, we will try something else.

It has been interesting seeing her response this week. She was crying Tuesday night and then immediately stood up and put her hand over her heart. The baseball game on television had started playing the national anthem. With tears in her eyes, mourning her mother, she broke from grief to stand for the anthem, even one playing on television. Because that is what she feels you are supposed to do.

She is an interesting girl, this daughter of mine.

There is a lot going on in her head that she never allows to slip out. She has her own words that sometimes sound like ours but don't always have the same definition. And her primary translator is gone. She is now stuck with me in that role, whether either of us are ready for the change.

She is playing a song, "Tears of the Lonely", performed by Don Williams. I thought it was an interesting choice, so I looked up the lyrics.

> Faded pictures, yellow from time
> Well-worn memories of days gone by
> Needing someone and nobody's there
> These are the things
> Broken dreams are made of,
> Lord they're everywhere.

Oh, the tears of the lonely
Keep falling all the time,
Tears of the lonely
Never dry.

Another nighttime that just never ends
A helpless longing for what might have been
Another morning to face all alone
These are the things
Broken dreams are made of,
They go on and on.

Oh, the tears of the lonely
Keep falling all the time,
Tears of the lonely
Never dry.

I'd say, translator or not, based on her song selection her words are pointed.

The tears of the lonely. Yep, she is communicating with us just fine.

We are at the cemetery.

The timing isn't ideal. I agonized over how to handle this. Madison has had an awful week. But Friday was good. She was happy. She was almost herself again.

We are back in Livingston for a funeral service for Hannah's uncle. At one point this week, I wondered if we would make this trip. Hannah is in the same cemetery.

It was still one of those decisions you tend to over-analyze. I have tried to do the right thing during this process, even when it is hard. But when the decision impacts others, it is a different concept entirely. Especially someone as vulnerable as Madison is right now.

So, before anyone else got to the cemetery, when only the birds and squirrels were watching, we made a practice run.

We brought some roses. Madison took them and put them on her mother's grave. I asked her who was there, and she solemnly said, "Mommy".

I asked if there was anything she wanted to talk to her mom about? She stood there, silent. So, I started. And like last visit, she repeated my words.

We talked about going to the beach. We told her about visiting our friends Lance, Molly and their daughter Lucy. We told her about going to see her aunt Laurie and her family. And that MiMi had been staying some at our house. And how all of these people had been so nice to us. I named names. Madison repeated them.

I paused.

"Blonde highlights," a voice spoke out.

"Yes, we have an appointment Thursday for blonde highlights. How could I forget to mention something so important?" I'm sure her mother smiled.

Madison was strong throughout. Her voice didn't crack. Her eyes didn't water. Her dad can't say the same. We have flipped roles again. My helper is back.

She will be fine today. Our girl has remarkable strength.

Even when she has to do the hard thing, the right thing.

Tonight, felt different.

We had been out of town as the hurricane hit near our gulf coast home. That said, we had our own storm to deal with at the cemetery that turned out milder than expected. After a rocky Sunday morning and then a detour back to Livingston to claim someone's pink iPhone left under her uncle's guest room pillow, we made it home.

We picked up the limbs Hurricane Nate had left behind. Otherwise, he was kind to us.

Madison had a bath and came and sat at the kitchen table. I'm not always great at hints but I think she was expecting me to feed her.

Since Hannah passed, many of our meals have been taken care of. Some wonderful families have basically adopted us by bringing us food a couple of times per week. We warm leftovers the next day. My mom has been here some to help with many things, meals included. And many weekends we have been elsewhere where food was handled by others.

I tell you this because I haven't had to cook. This isn't a new thing. Over the years, Hannah handled practically all of our home meals. Baring a grill or smoker session, it was all her. It wasn't that I couldn't, I just didn't. It was another thing I allowed her to do because she was better at it than I was.

In the past weeks, I have microwaved but done nothing on the stove or in the oven. Instead of finding something to nuke, tonight I decided to use some of those groceries in the refrigerator. Madison and I looked through the fridge and she grabbed some bacon.

Who doesn't like bacon? Bacon, I can handle.

We looked for something that would go with bacon. There were six eggs in a carton. Bingo.

Y'all, we cooked bacon. Then we cooked eggs. Me and my helper. She added cheese.

And you know, it wasn't bad. Madison ate. I ate. Then we cleaned up afterward.

It felt different tonight. It felt good to do for myself. To do for Madi. To do with Madi. To not feel like a fish out of water. Small victories.

While we cooked, we asked Alexa to play Taylor Swift. Madison sang along. I have missed her singing.

In these past six weeks, so many of our activities have been forced and as a result left everyone exhausted. We haven't had a lot of singing. We haven't had a lot of feelings of belonging. Tonight, we had both. It was the first time in a long time I relaxed and just did something that felt easy; natural.

Who knows what tomorrow will bring? Another storm could be imminent. But tonight, was a night of the new normal. Yes, someone was missing. But we got through it with both a smile and a song. And dinner. Don't forget the dinner.

Author's note: Here is a story written a few years ago about my grandmother, Elizabeth Etheridge.

She never says good-bye.

She is now 91 years old. Up until a few years ago, she could outwork anyone you care to mention.

"Us folks out in the country just do as we can," she said modestly. "I just grunt and go."

She has slowed down a bit, but the house is still spotless. Drop in anytime, it is always organized. And it feels warm and welcoming.

These days you can almost taste the homemade biscuits as you walk through the door. Memories are funny like that. A smell reminds you of a day from your childhood and a place can fill your heart with warmth or churn your guts into jello.

She lost her husband over three years ago. She admits she is lonely. After all, they were married over 65 years. He came home from World War II and they made a nice life for themselves in rural Alabama. They raised two sons and four grandkids who never had to wonder about their devotion.

"I miss him more now than I ever have," she admits. "I don't know why it's so but I guess because the shock has worn off."

"Sometimes, it seems like he is just out and will be home from work any minute now." Her voice trails off, "I sure miss him."

Her church is important to her. She wants all her family to be reunited together some day. Her prayers are not like many of ours, which often seem like hopes and wishes. She asks for something and expects it to happen. Just like you or I expect the light to come on when we flip the switch, that's the way she feels about her prayers. Her kind of faith, the kind that seems uncommon in today's world, has served her well.

These days she is mostly self-sufficient but has someone come stay with her at night. She wants to remain at home and hang on to that routine as long as possible. After all, she has lived in that same house since the 1950s. The thought of leaving that familiar day-to-day is scary. But much of the day is spent in solitude with way too much time inside her head.

So, she wears out the telephone. Like she is running for office, she talks to anyone and everyone. If you call her number, odds are you will get a busy signal. Yep, those still exist. There's no call waiting, cell phones, or texts in her world. Just a big black phone that weighs nearly as much as she does.

With her trusty weapon, she gets the scoop on everyone. She rarely misses a birthday call to anyone she knows. If you are sick, a call and maybe a card. She checks on the "old people" – forgetting that label might also apply to her. On her own birthday, she said as soon as one call ended, the phone was ringing again so another began. She is genuine, and people respond to her.

And when those conversations end, she never says goodbye.

One day I asked about the story behind a question she had never before been asked. Why did she not echo back the good byes at the close of the conversation?

"I guess a long time ago I got in the habit of not saying bye and it kind of grew on me," she said, thinking a little more before adding. "I used to never think about saying bye because I am going to talk to you again."

That kind of resonates with me. The hope that there is always a next chat, a new story, or another day to discuss the upcoming birthday, wedding, or funeral.

As our conversation drew to close, she said, "You know we love you."

"Yes maam, I do. We love you too."

"And Mark."

"Maam?"

"Bye, Mark."

The first half mile was fast for this distance. I knew I should slow down. The faster my mind raced, the faster my legs churned.

I am one of those people who have trouble slowing their brains down. That makes me good at multi-tasking; good at adjusting from the last idea to the next one. Focusing on a single item can be a problem. That is how I have lived for much of my 45 years.

I have run this six-mile neighborhood route hundreds of times. My pace has now slowed back to target. I wanted to average nine-minute miles. So, I glance at the pace on my Garmin watch every minute or so. It is easy to lose your way chasing rainbows.

My mind switches from topic to topic. I have headphones playing Amazon Music "adult pop". This is something I would have never listened to before, a suggestion from a friend to mix things up. It is mostly background noise to the "idea ping-pong tournament" inside my head.

There is a hill coming up. I lift my knees a little higher. Increase my cadence a bit. My mind drifts to a problem from work. Then just as quickly, I am thinking about Madison's senior portraits. I need to put my order in today. And I'm up the hill, still on pace.

Hey, is this Adele singing? She is really talented. I have heard but never really listened, if you get my meaning. If she and Chris Stapleton ever did a duet album, I might listen to it non-stop all day.

I am out on the neighborhood main road now. Cars whiz by. I hop up and down from the street to the median. A squirrel runs away. He is probably wondering why I am running. So, do I sometimes. My mind drifts again.

Madison was happy yesterday. I would look over and she would just be smiling. What a difference a week makes. Like her Dad, her moods can flip from zero to sixty as quick as a corvette. She has been through a hellish six weeks. It was good to see that smile.

Out of nowhere a dog comes to greet me. It is small, fluffy and yapping for all it is worth. I keep on route and it smartly moves aside in an impromptu game of chicken. I think about our pets that we re-homed after this happened. How would Hannah feel about that? Surely, she would understand. My plate was full enough. Still, it makes me a little sad.

I'm now about mile four. I see another runner up ahead. She has a decent pace. I look at my watch and figure I will catch her in around a minute. I pick up my pace a bit. I want the distraction, the challenge.

"On your left," I say seconds before I fly by. She never acknowledges. After I pass, I look down at my watch. Forty-three seconds. I guess I overestimated her pace. But it got me out of my head for nearly a minute. I welcomed the respite.

About a mile later, I noticed I am off pace having slowed considerably from target. I had been thinking about Hannah. That typically either really picks me up or drags me to a crawl. This time it tied weights to my ankles.

I have learned so much about her, and myself for that matter, since her passing. This weighs heavily on me. I want to let it slide through my fingers but I'm not yet ready. So, I keep pushing the rock up the hill. It is heavy.

I snap back, change my mindset. I know I have to. Now I need to push again to make up for the slower pace. My stride lengthens. My knees pump higher. I focus on breathing. This is comfortable. I know what I am doing here. I need this familiarity … on this route where I could run blindfolded. I breeze up a steep hill like it is flat. Focused, determined, I am in the last mile now.

I tell myself, "You don't know when you will get to run again. Make the most of this." A man walking his dog yells hello to me. I wave without breaking stride.

My mind is busy again, bouncing from topic to topic. I am still pushing hard to make up the lost time, something I am unable to do in other parts of my life.

I make the final turn, there is a quarter mile left. I push harder. This is something I can still control in a world where it now seems I am always reacting.

A Taylor Swift song comes on. Of course, I think of Madison. My pace gets even quicker. I push. I barrel into the driveway and hit the stop button. The Garmin says right at 54 minutes. That is six miles at a nine-minute pace. Right on target after all.

Today, I made up for lost time. At least this is possible in one aspect of life.

My mind stops for a minute. I feel calm. I feel accomplishment. All I did was go for a run.

And now, back to real life.

Here we are again. It is 3:23 AM and the insomnia has returned.

I have tossed and turned, turned and tossed. I have counted sheep, goats, cows, and 487 jack-a-lopes. I have counted backwards from 100, in seven different languages (not really, I barely know one). I have taken so many deep breaths I may now be an honorary yogi.

Why tonight? I had a good run this morning. I worked all day. There was a strength workout in the evening. There was a nice conversation with a new friend. It was a full day. The adrenaline should have exited by now. But here we are, staring at that damn light fixture again.

The bedroom lights are on now. There is no use pretending. The alarm will go off in a couple of hours. Madison will need to get ready for school. She will be raring to go.

Our girl loves school. And from all indications, many at her school love her as well. She is a charmer, even with her limited social skills. And so many gravitate to her sweet spirit.

But I lay here, waiting. I could work out again. I could hop on the treadmill. I could read. These are things I have been doing to fill time during normal waking hours. If this keeps up, I will be the fittest book nerd in the county. Then again, I may be the only one.

I haven't really started back with television yet, with the exception of live sports. My attention span doesn't allow it. There are so many adaptations. So much loneliness time to fill.

Hannah and I were together for over 25 years. I talked to her every day throughout the day, saw her almost every day. Told her I loved her at the close at every conversation. This is an adjustment in so many ways.

There is a big hole. Some can be filled by other people. Lots of great people are trying really hard and it is appreciated. The large things are taken care of. I have plenty of family and friends to discuss major topics with. What I miss are the minor conversations.

"How was your day?"

"Did your company make their monthly numbers?"

"What should we get as a gift for a first birthday party?"

"Are these pants too big?"

"Don't you have enough shoes?"

I took those smaller topics for granted. Just having that connection with someone to throw out an odd topic and get an odd response. And it not feel odd.

People have asked about the hardest part of this ordeal?

Putting the initial shock out of the equation along with figuring out the whole single, autism parent thing, the next hardest part has been filling my "free time" when Madison is asleep or busy.

As I mentioned, there is a hole I haven't yet learned how to fill. There is too much time alone with my thoughts and not enough time connecting – with someone or something. Anything.

As bad as last week was, Madison is having a great week. That is such a weight off of all of us. However, as challenging as it was dealing with her grief last week, it gave me something to hyper-focus on. Without it, I am left to deal with my own dilemma.

And apparently back here staring at the damn ceiling.

I have been sleeping better. I'd say five or six hours most nights. It doesn't sound like progress, but it is. We have come a long way, me and my support group. Tonight, is a reminder there is still ground to cover.

Holes to fill.

Now what about that party gift?

The moment of truth came as the chair spun around. We were three hours into this and our girl isn't known for her patience.

Yes, it had been a long wait measured in repetitions of "five more minutes" obsessively chanted about every ten seconds. I wish I was exaggerating.

Some waits are worth it.

Our stylist Amelia had spent the evening putting blonde highlights into Madison's hair. She also shampooed and trimmed our diva's locks. Anything worthwhile is worth waiting for, someone once said. But whoever said that probably wasn't faced with coming up with new comebacks for a barrage from the "five more minutes" brigade.

What if it wasn't blonde enough? I mean, she knows what highlights are but in the back of your mind you couldn't help but wonder if she wanted it really blonde like her mom. That would make a lot of sense, right? Or what if she just didn't like it? I hear women can be kind of picky about their hair (I'm sure that's just folklore).

After she struggled last week, we used "blonde highlights" as a target, a carrot dangling out there for future happiness. No matter how bad she felt, there was something to look forward to that she cared about. One of the messages I have lived and learned the past six weeks is how important hope is to this process. You need something to cling to, something that you hope will bring relief to your melancholy spirit. Often the anticipation is better than the reality and that isn't a reflection on the results. She needed this appointment and she needed to know something good was coming.

I just really hoped it would turn out that she liked it.

And the thing is, she would tell you if she didn't. We don't really spare feelings at times around here. Madison was asked if she liked the chili someone made her a few weeks back? Her answer, "Yuck". Right to the cook's face. So, if the hair didn't turn out, I was a bit apprehensive how the sideline reporter's postgame interview with the gruff coach would turn out.

When she woke up this morning, I asked her what today was. She didn't answer Thursday or October 12 or anything that she might normally answer. Her answer? "Blonde highlights."

It was never far from her thoughts.

We were about to get our verdict.

The chair spun around, and our girl got her first glimpse. Dad crouched a few feet away, like a cheetah lying in the weeds waiting for the right moment to pounce on the gazelle. Madison soaked in the image staring back at her in the mirror. That young lady looked much different than the one that strolled into Salon 31 for a 6 pm appointment. She processed … now it was my turn to not want to wait anymore.

The corners of her mouth turned up. Our girl, who had been stone-faced much of the evening, beamed. That light that had been waiting to shine was glowing like a row of midnight jack-o-lanterns. She really liked it.

And at that point it was one of those occasions where you wish time would stop – and just let this moment linger a bit.

We walked over to the selfie station. Madison posed for us. I don't know if I have ever seen her smile so radiantly. Her mother's smile shone through and I thought about how proud Hannah would be at that very moment. We snapped a few more photos, paid and went to the car.

The two of us buckled in and we sat there a minute. I thought about all the hell she and I had been through the past six weeks. I thought about all of the uncertainty I had wondering if I could make her happy without her mom to guide us both. But then I thought about that smile. That beautiful, window-to-the-soul smile that demonstrated her genuine happiness.

And I remembered one of the first things we said after Hannah passed.

"I got this."

I wasn't sure I really believed it. But I sure as heck said it. I'm a little closer to believing it.

Yep, Hannah. We got this. At least we do for today.

All you need to do is check out that smile.

———————————————

"Momma ... no way."

Sometimes a girl needs her mom.

Madison knows her mom is gone. Her calls still slip out. She immediately corrects herself with a "nope" or "no way". She dabs the corners of her eyes. That is as far as I can get her to take the conversation.

We went to their spot for breakfast Saturday. And it was their spot. I had been a couple of times as their guest. On days where Madison went to work with Hannah, they would go before work to a coffee shop and get a frou-frou coffaletta (or something like that) and an equally fancy breakfast sandwich. The two of us tried it for the first time this weekend and it seemed to go OK. This bridge with Dad playing Mom's role went well. That isn't always the case.

We stayed at home the rest of Saturday. I got some stuff done around the house and then tried to watch football. You may recall our last weekend at home didn't go well. Madison struggled and as a result, so did I. This one was better, although she had a hard time in the afternoon. We made a trip to the grocery store, snagged some oatmeal cookies and bluebell ice cream and that helped us get through the evening. Madison can sometimes be bribed with sweets and I'm not above using that to push aside a meltdown.

We went to the Shrimp Festival in Gulf Shores on Sunday. We moved to Daphne in 2010 and have been each year since. Some years I would take off from work on Friday and Hannah and I would go, just the two of us while Madison was in school. It was a quick date in a relationship that didn't have nearly enough of them. Most years we would go back later in the weekend and take Madison.

This year was our shortest stint there. It started fine. Madison picked out a soft-shell crab basket and we found somewhere to sit in the shade. She enjoyed it. I thought the day was going well.

We tried to walk around and look at the vendors' wares. This was more of a "Mommy" role, apparently. As we walked, I tried to get her to slow down. Hannah would often get frustrated as Madison basically raced down the aisles through the crowd. As a result, Hannah often had to window shop in fast forward, if at all. I suppose when I asked Madi to slow down, the words triggered something with her.

She started to get agitated. There was a group of bright clothes over on the left. She headed for them. I followed. As she got there, "shirt", she shouted. "Shirt, shirt, shirt."

There might have been 500 shirts in front of us.

She then stopped at a bench and said, "sad, heartbroken". That has been her code for thinking of her mom.

I had pushed too far.

The shopping part of this day was too reminiscent of her mother. She was struggling. Mom was supposed to be here to help pick her out a shirt. Dad would just screw this up. She was probably right.

We sat together as I tried to assess the next move. Behind us was a smaller booth with fewer shirts. Maybe this would be less overwhelming? We steered over and found a shirt she liked. She was still a bit agitated, but at least she had found her a shirt.

She wanted pants now. I mean, they do go with shirts. I get it. So, we left and headed to the outlet in Foley, which was another risky move. This was another place the three of us went. I don't think I had ever been there without Hannah and I'm sure Madison hadn't.

We were able to find pants. It was hard not to think about past trips there; who we bumped into and our shared experiences over the years. But she handled it fine.

Madison is missing her mom. The weekends at home are going to be a problem for some time, I fear.

I have been trying. As dads go, I do OK. As for replacing her mom, I'm not up for the task. Sure, I can get her ready for school, take her for hair appointments and get her fed, but I am not able to provide the same experiences Madison has grown accustomed to having.

I am searching for the balance between continuing the traditions she shared with her mother and avoiding the ones that may be too painful. She can't tell me, not really. So, I am making educated guesses, reading reactions and adjusting on the fly. These are activities she enjoyed. She has lost so much. I want to keep some of them going where I can.

There are going to be days where she is "sad, heartbroken". Days when she calls for her mom and then corrects herself. I can't fix that. No one can.

Because I am not her momma. No way.

I am watching baseball. It is the playoffs. I haven't watched this much playoff baseball in years.

I don't have to share the television viewing anymore. Madison is in her room watching her own shows … which isn't baseball, by the way. I am alone in what was once a shared bedroom that is now solely mine.

I saw a commercial for The Walking Dead season premiere. Hannah didn't miss an episode. So, a few years back I started watching it with her each week. Lord knows she had watched enough sports with me. And after she got me caught up, I started to look forward to it each week. It gave us something to talk about after the episodes.

I think I am going to watch the premiere Sunday night. I don't know who I will talk about it with. Here is something else that we will figure out as we go.

That is where I am right now. I know the holidays will be dreadful. But since I own a calendar I know when they are coming and can sort of prepare. A commercial for a series we watched together just pops in, smacks you in the gut, and is gone as quick as it came. I never expected that to bother me but that funny feeling in your gut just refuses to depart.

It has been seven weeks. Some days I feel adjusted, almost normal. We are getting our routines in place and some people are still helping out, long after the shock of the moment has passed. This still both impresses and surprises me. Those people sure have a lot of compassion.

For the most part, the hard days come on days where Madison struggles. I am forced to deal with it — there are no avoidance mind games allowed if she is struggling.

This morning she was sitting at the table eating Frosted Flakes for breakfast. I was getting our lunches together while the coffee maker popped and gurgled. I heard a sniffle and then a wail.

"Heartbroken," I heard.

My shoulders just sunk. I couldn't avoid my body language. I was doing fine up until then but hearing her sadness flipped the mood completely.

I walked over to her and we embraced. She needed that hug. All I can say, "I know, baby. I know. I miss her too."

"Mommy, gone. Sad. Heartbroken."

Those are a lot of words for her to string together. To her, it had to seem like she had just finished a speech. And I have never heard words whose message was any clearer.

She immediately broke away and ran to her room. She had something on her mind. She came back seconds later, wearing her "Hannah necklace".

Madison cried a little more on the couch as we waited for the school bus. I talked to her about her mom. We talked about how pretty her blonde highlights are and how much her mom would have liked them. Madison smiled. We talked about how good she was doing helping her dad. And how we are helping each other because we have to. She seemed to need that chat – that reassurance that she was doing a good job.

I get that. No matter how things are going I still feel like I am playing a character. That any day now the act will end, and I will go back to my old life, where I was comfortable and typically knew what I was doing.

Instead, I continue to pretend.

By the time she bounded off to the bus, she was fine. She is resilient.

I was drained. The drama sapped my energy. The work day awaited.

Tonight, we had leftovers for dinner. She commented on them with "yum" and "delicious". I think she meant it. She was reassuring me, this time. Our girl.

We did the dishes together. After she got ready for bed, I am left to myself. This is the worst. In this bedroom that I used to share.

The baseball game is on television, but I am not really watching. Alone again. And my thoughts begin to focus. I keep coming back to words eloquently spoken that need no improvement.

Sad, heartbroken.

Author's note: October 20 was my grandfather's birthday. I wrote this about the final days of his life as he battled dementia. Only a couple of people have ever seen this prior to publication.

He is driving a truck.

It is late at night. He hasn't been in a driver's seat in years. His mind isn't his own.

He is shifting with his arms. His legs, unsteady while upright, are working the gas and brake. His son looks on, worried, seated beside the bed.

Dementia, the doctors call it. It has taken his mind. He isn't the same man who used to take his grandchildren to ballgames, grow an overflowing garden and offer the shirt off his back to strangers. Seeing him this way hurts a special kind of pain.

He can't be left alone. And not just because of his midnight imaginary drives in his pickup.

He doesn't recognize his wife, his sons, his friends. He can get mean. He was never mean. This may be the cruelest part of all for onlookers.

His Sundowners make the nights dreadful. His grandson doesn't want to see him this way.

The grandson tells a story about a ballgame, a gridiron contest in a raucous college stadium years ago when the younger man was a teen. The wave started across the stadium. Slowly, section by section, people rose and waved. The grandfather was excited to participate in something he had only seen on television. In this case, he was like the child and the teen ignored the pending situation, too cool to be bothered.

As the wave came closer, anticipation mounted. Then it was their turn. One of them stood, the other stayed seated in all his teenage coolness.

The older man glared at him, not out of anger or frustration. It was disappointment. That look seared into the youngster's brain. He sees it during his own midnight rides. He would love another chance to stand and cheer. And wave.

That opportunity has passed.

The sun rises in the bedroom and a glimpse of the normal personality peeks through, even though the man might not recognize people he has known for decades.

"Do you know Stanley Etheridge?" the old man asked.

"I do," said the visitor sitting beside his bed.

"That's my son," the old man said with a familiar smile.

The visitor choked back his response. The room was quiet for a moment. How do you respond to that?

"He's a good boy," the old man said.

Out of all of their father/son talks, this one might have been the most genuine.

———————————

Years ago, when I started running road races, people used to ask, "did you win?"

I always laughed and explained, "no, I will never win a race. I just run competing against myself to try to improve each time."

Because I never thought I would win an actual race. I joked with Hannah, and I wondered if she was listening or rather tuned me out when the subject flipped to running, "that if ALL of the fast people would just stay home, I would have a chance".

I guess they all stayed home Saturday.

Did you ever have one of those days where there really isn't any explanation? That things just sort of drop into place? A day that makes you question if there was a higher power involved? Someone mentioned it can be called a "God wink".

Madison and I went to my Dad's house in Thomasville. I haven't been able to run as much as I used to and since Madi could stay with them, I decided to go for a run. I contemplated just starting at the front door and heading out from there. But at the last minute, I changed my mind, got in the car and drove downtown. My reasoning was that I had not been down there for over a decade and what better way to see what has changed than a tour on foot.

So, I went for a run. About three miles in, I noticed a table set up in front of a building. It looked a lot like a race setup, but I thought, "Mark, everything isn't about running just because you are out for a run."

Still, as I got closer, I overheard a lady ask "here comes a runner! Are you running in the 5K?"

I was surprised but thought, "sure. I'm game". I didn't have any money with me, so I ran back to my car for my wallet and then drove back to the race start site to get registered. This would be the first race after losing Hannah. She was always supportive of my running, at least in my presence anyway. We would usually talk before the race and then I would text her how I did after finishing. I would carry on about pacing or strategy or what body part was nagging me. She pretended to be interested and was convincing. I didn't have her receptive ear today.

I wondered as the race was about to start if this was some sort of sign, that I just stumbled into a 5K. I looked around the starting line and chuckled to myself wondering if this was the day all the fast people stayed home.

The race started, and a young boy took the lead. He was going out too fast, in my opinion so I didn't match his start. Over the years I have started in the lead pack many times, but I always slowed later in the race. I have learned not to start too fast.

The boy slowed at the first hill and I passed him. I had no idea how close the next racer was. At a turn about a mile into the race, I snuck a peek behind me.

No one was particularly close. At this point it occurred to me that if I didn't blow up (pace improperly), I would likely win this race. So, I focused on keeping an easy pace. I told myself to cruise until the last half mile and then hammer the final leg.

As I got to that final half mile, I thought about all the races I had run since my first 5K years ago. How I had resigned myself to just improving, but never really being competitive. And how Hannah had sacrificed so much of her own free time to support me through the years. And I pushed hard for that final kick.

A group of kids came out to cheer as I neared the finish. I gave high fives and exchanged smiles. I crossed the finish line, stopped my Garmin at 22:16 and accepted the congratulations from my new-found fans.

After each race, I would always text Hannah how I did. She would usually send back a, "YAY!", because even a slow time for me was impressive to her. She was so supportive. I sent her one final post-race text.

"You aren't going to believe this, but I won a 5K today. Wish I could tell you all about it. Love you." It felt so strange adding her name to the TO: field and then hitting send.

I doubled back and cheered on the next wave of finishers. Then later on went back to travel the last fifty yards with the final finisher. Everyone needs a cheering section regardless of pace.

In the aftermath, there was my now familiar feeling of faking my way through recent events. I acted like I knew how to win a race. I didn't.

Since her passing, there have been so many new experiences. But this one? How do you explain stumbling into a 5K while on a regular training run where no one knew where I planned to run? And then winning my first ever race in the first one I have tried since her death?

I collected my trophy and the prize for winning, a $50 gift card to the local steakhouse Big Mike's and headed back to Dad's. As I walked in and explained where I had been the last few hours, they explained Madi had been repeating a request to go out to eat all morning ... to Big Mike's Steakhouse.

I'm not the most religious guy. And I'm not sure how I feel about the supernatural. But the way all of this came together this morning, it felt like a setup. Like someone, or something, had put these different outcomes in my path today.

It has been a rough eight weeks, but I had a really good day.

A road race came to me. I got to win a race and also

try to give some support back to others. We got Madison a nice meal with a gift card. All of that came together.

It happened because all of the fast people stayed home. Maybe she was listening after all.

The dresses sat in the closet. Out of sight, out of mind. Forgotten.

It has been eight weeks. Fifty-six days where the sun did indeed come up. Most of the time I am fine. I'm laughing, making others laugh, getting work done and making sure Madison's needs are met. During those times I am me, only a better, more productive (if not more exhausted) version.

Then something happens. A certain song, smell or image. And it hurts.

The cooler weather brought one on. Hannah hated being cold. We have so many throws and blankets. Each year I would get her another one for Christmas because it was always a gift she would like. It was an easy secondary gift. We have dozens. As the temps dropped this week, I went into a closet and pulled a couple out. The same closet where I had stashed many of her dresses, jackets and tops.

Out of sight or mind no longer.

I pulled out some old photos. After a few minutes, I put them back.

There are lots of Christmas photos in there and to be honest, I am dreading these next few months. Our wedding anniversary is November 23. This year that falls on Thanksgiving Day, just a brutal double-dip. Then comes my birthday, Christmas, Hannah's birthday, Madison's birthday and Valentines. None will be festive, despite the best of intentions. If I could fast forward to mid-February, I probably would.

And that bothers me ... to look that far ahead. Obviously, we aren't promised tomorrow. We all got a harsh lesson on August 30th. Each day should be a gift. Wouldn't we all cherish one more day with someone who ran out of sunrises?

My mom is taking the closet contents back with her. They really will be out of sight from now on. As we were loading them up, I made the mistake of looking at a couple of them. It is just clothes, right? But my eyes got wet and that familiar lump in my throat returned. It had been on vacation, apparently, but came back to work with a double espresso and new PowerPoint slides. I would like to send it away again.

Now the closet is empty, ready to fill with something. Life is like that, I guess. Just a series of empty closets and we get to choose how to fill them. Ideally, you fill them with happy memories but sometimes you just need to put things away to deal with later. That's the cool thing about an empty closet, there is room for you to fill based on your needs at the time.

Like so many things today, I don't know how I should fill this empty closet. Life has been a whirlwind during the last eight weeks. So many decisions. So much second-guessing. Despite best attempts by many, loneliness has become an opponent.

In some ways, I'd like to fill a few boxes with regrets and missed opportunities, put them high on a shelf and then padlock the door. But there are lessons from those that feed me moving forward, a desire to not repeat those same mistakes as opportunities emerge.

Make the call. Send the text. Say out loud what once went unsaid. Give the compliment and make sure they know you mean it. Swallow the unproductive, antagonistic comment. Don't dismiss the new idea. Learn from mistakes and more importantly, figure out a way to apply the acquired knowledge.

Yeah, I'd like to pack all that hurt up out of sight, out of mind. But not today. I want to feel. I want to grow. I want to do what I didn't before. The hurt fuels growth.

That closet, well, it is empty. And how we fill it is up

to us.

Steak, not really.

Fish, well, it has to flake perfect.

Pork? Only if it is bacon or pulled apart – not cut.

Notice the taste is not as important as the texture.

But oysters, one of the weirdest food textures on the planet? Enter her in the all-you-can-eat competition and move out of the way.

It all started years ago. Hannah and I loved to go to New Orleans and when we did, we would always order raw oysters. I don't remember my first raw oyster, but it is most certainly a leap of faith. It doesn't even look like food. But we guys tend to do a lot of things that our girls want us to. And I liked it.

We never offered Madison any oysters. It was one of those things where mom and dad knew better. She had autism. She had a picky diet. She struggled with food textures. So, there was no way she would like oysters.

But she would watch intently as we put the cocktail sauce together. The ketchup, the horseradish, the Saltines. We made a production out of it and she soaked it in. On one particular trip, she really stared. Hannah offered her a crackered raw oyster and she looked hard but passed. We laughed, "yep, thought so."

We finished our meal and remarked how interested young Madison seemed in those creatures on the shells. Well, they do look kind of odd.

The next time we ordered oysters ... we didn't order enough.

She had been apparently thinking about it and summoned her courage for her leap of faith. And she scaled the wall.

We fixed the first oyster. Hannah saw her staring, smiled at me and said, "I guess we are going to do this again?"

As the cracker moved toward Madi, her hand snatched it and stuffed it into her mouth. We gasped. Then we expected to be cleaning a mess off the floor.

That slimy texture. That horseradish nose-tickle. This was definitely coming back out.

But it didn't. I wish we had video of our faces. We must have sat with our jaws open. She chewed. I suppose that was for show. Or maybe it was the cracker. But she swallowed the oyster. And we just watched, dumbfounded – awaiting the next act of the show.

So, I handed her the one I had made. And she took it. And it disappeared. This continued. She kept eating them, so we kept handing them to her. She was hooked. It was love at first bite.

To prove this was no fluke, we went back to another oyster place soon after that. We wondered if she just got caught up in the moment or if this was a new thing. She devoured them.

Now, everyone who dines with Madison at an oyster restaurant has a story. The girl loves oysters.

She has overcome some of her texture issues. She now likes a high dollar steak, among other things. But with all of her maturation, her changes, the most unlikely delicacy has remained one of her favorites.

Obviously, she has changed a great deal in the past eight weeks. She helps keep the house in order. She has tried many different foods that prior to August 30, she would have just ignored.

We went out for dinner Friday. She picked the place. Guess what she picked?

Yep, oysters. And she devoured them. She was so excited as they came out. So much has changed in the last two months. It was nice for both of us to find something stable, that feels the same as it has for years.

Like old times, I fixed them for her. She enjoyed them. This makes us both happy. We have each lost so many of our traditions, our history, our shared experiences. I think we are finding ways to cling to some that are sustainable.

Even the unlikely ones, the ones no one believed when they started. Like the texture-sensitive girl who loves oysters.

I have tried to write this story several times. Each time before this one, it has ended with a "CTRL+A, delete". The topic is a hard one for me. Another lost opportunity. Another regret. Another reminder of something I would just as soon forget.

I never really cared for Halloween. I suppose I inherited that. Neither of my parents are fans. But Hannah loved Halloween. She would sometimes dress up and make the holiday really fun for herself and Madison.

She did that without me. While I didn't discourage her verbally, certainly my lack of interest was apparent. We like what we like, and I didn't like Halloween.

Which leads to a story. It was Saturday evening, August 5th of this year. This was three and half weeks before Hannah passed away. The three of us were at home and we decided to have a movie night. Hannah and Madison picked Beauty and the Beast. As they watched, I mostly played on my phone.

About halfway through the movie, Hannah looked over and saw I wasn't watching. She barked, "this is my favorite movie. Can you at least pretend to be interested?"

I was taken aback. I didn't know this was her favorite movie. And I really didn't know it was important to her that I watch with her. I felt bad. Like a scolded child, I put my phone away and watched the rest of the movie.

After the movie ended, I got my phone back out. I had an idea. I wanted to make it up to her.

So, I went online and ordered a Halloween costume for the Beast. I planned to surprise her at Halloween this year. Not only would I be in costume, I would be a character from her favorite movie. And I would be embracing something she was interested in. Oh, the best laid plans.

A few days later the package was on the doorstep. She was home when it arrived and texted me that I received something. I told her it was a surprise and when I got home, I hid the unopened package in the closet.

I had not given it much additional thought until after she passed. I went into the closet to get my suit for her service and there it was, a different kind of suit, the one I wanted for a surprise. I never got the chance to show her, to make it up to her.

Folks, I hope she snooped to see what the surprise package was. She was naturally curious. I hope she figured out what I had planned. And I hope she smiled when she saw it. And I really hope she would have liked my surprise this coming Tuesday for Halloween.

I wanted to do something nice. To encourage an interest instead of discourage. To try to right a series of wrongs.

But I ran out of time.

I don't know why I am sharing this story. It hurts. I don't enjoy going through this again.

It feels like it had to happen though. Halloween is coming, whether anyone wants it to, whether you enjoy it or not.

And no, I won't be a beauty like when Hannah

dressed up as Cinderella. But I can be a beast.

Her Beast.

They were waiting on the street when I got home at 5:30. There was a steady stream of short, costumed people at our door for a couple of hours.

I now see why Hannah would set up on the front steps with a table, Madison at her side, and would buy enough candy where she wouldn't run out. She was nicer than me. Everywhere we have lived, it has been a Halloween candy buffet. Hannah loved that part of Halloween. Seeing all the cuteness, the little monsters, and greeting people. She loved to brag on the sweet ones and complain (to me, after they left) about the rude ones.

I miss her today.

This is one of those days I feared would be hard. I got up this morning dreading it. Everyone was talking about their trick-or-treating stories at work today. I volunteered a couple as well. I could tell I was losing my composure a little bit – and I had been pretty steady for the past few weeks.

On the drive home, a song came on the radio that brought all that had been lurking below the surface bubbling to the top. It was Cole Swindell's, "You

Should Be Here". There's a phrase in there:

"It's one of those moments, that's got your name
written all over it;
And you know that if I had just one wish it'd
Be that you didn't have to miss this
You should be here."

My chest sunk with that familiar heavy weight, a
feeling that has been my wingman the last two
months. My eyes got wet and what had been
building all week heading into today came out in a
flurry. The song ended. I switched to a podcast. And I
regrouped. And rallied.

The other part of the Halloween dynamic was how
would Madison handle tonight?

We had some work done on our house today and I
was finishing up with the crew as the early wave of
trick-or-treaters arrived. In fact, I saw a family leaving
the house and tried to stop them.

"Oh no, your daughter took care of us," the man said.
Oh really?

Madison had decided it was up to her to manage the
candy allotment this year. My helper. She was
enthusiastic and authoritative.

So, I watched her, guided her, and negotiated our

candy disbursement strategy. She wanted control. She picked what each kid got. She put it in their bag. And they got one piece. That's right, only one of her choosing. My daughter, the candy Nazi.

Me, I want the candy gone as soon as possible so I can stop handing it out. So, I just lower the bowl and let them pick what they want. Some grab one or two. Some grab a handful. One kid tried the "scrape it into the sack" method but I was wise to his plan and intervened. Not my first time at the door, kid. Madison wasn't eager to alter her structured method. I don't know where she gets that stubbornness from, but she might have been 5'3", blonde and looked cute in a Cinderella costume.

I was worried about how Madison would handle Halloween. She did great. I think in hindsight my preoccupation with her made me underestimate how I would be affected. These family outing types of holidays are going to be a challenge.

Even though I'm fighting it at times, I'm the sentimental type. As I got dressed this morning, I was thinking of Hannah. I put on the green shirt she liked – the one I said goodbye to her in. I had said before I would not wear it again but this morning, I just felt like wearing it. There are no rules to this. I haven't seen them anyway. So, I wore the shirt. I may wear it again. Or maybe I won't. Who the heck knows or cares but me anyway?

Tonight, kept me busy, which while annoying was probably good. There were stretches where we would sit down less than a minute before there was someone else at the door. Madison sprang into action with a keen eye on the inventory in that candy bowl. She chattered to the kids. She called some of them by their character names. And she made sure each of them got that piece of candy. A singular piece, Dad.

We made the best of it. Hannah, you would have enjoyed tonight.

Yes, you should be here.

"What is that noise? Is that groaning? Odd," the man thought to himself.

The noise continued. What is that? Then a moment of clarity hit … "Oh my God, that's me".

The New York City Marathon is Sunday. Two years ago, I was there. Wide-eyed, excited, confident, determined. Five hours later only the determination remained.

I can't help but think about that trip this week. Hannah traveled with me. Just the two of us. Together. Only the adults. Without a child.

This all started when I won the lottery.

No, not the Powerball. I won the lottery for an entry into the New York City Marathon.

I completed a few half-marathons and people kept asking about taking on a full marathon. I said if I was ever going to do one, it would be one with a lot of diversions to distract from the "right foot, left foot, repeat" repetitions of 26.2 miles. I saw a video of the New York City Marathon and made a flippant remark about running it. So, Hannah told me to sign up. She basically called my bluff.

For popular races like that one, you can't just sign up. To gain entry, you can raise money for charity, be fast enough to qualify (ha ha, not a chance) or enter a lottery where roughly 1-in-5 applicants are selected.

We decided to allow fate to decide. I would enter the lottery and if I got in, it was meant to be. That would mean I was supposed to run a marathon and I would do it in grand style. Neither of us really expected to be planning a trip to The Big Apple.

But of course, I got in. Hannah told me that this would be the one lottery I would win ... not the one with the life-changing moolah. I settled for a life-changing experience instead.

I downloaded a training plan and stuck to it pretty well. Everything was progressing until two weeks prior to the day when I tried to accelerate, and my calf locked up. I couldn't walk. Here it was, fifteen days before I had to run 26.2 and I couldn't put any weight on my left leg. I frantically called a sports medicine/chiropractor and limped in with my sob story.

He took a look at me and said, "Sir, calm down. You should still be able to run your race. Now, if you will please come out from under the table, we will get you fixed up."

Then he took out a metal tool and started poking and scraping my calf. He called it Graston technique and it felt like he was trying to get me to tell state secrets, or maybe Maw-Maw's biscuit recipe. I think I would have talked, y'all.

But it worked. I saw him every morning. I went from putting no weight on that leg Monday morning to a treadmill jog on Thursday to a five-mile run on Sunday. Ironically, my injured calf is about the only thing that didn't plague me once I got to New York City.

I was very excited about the trip. Hannah was a bit apprehensive; she wasn't eager to tackle navigating Manhattan. We had done a day trip into NYC early in our marriage. I was consulting in New Jersey. She flew up and stayed over a weekend. We took the train into Manhattan and spent the day in the City. It didn't go well. We really didn't have a plan – just wandered aimlessly to a few tourist traps. We argued. When we got back to New Jersey she flew home early. That was her reference point and she understandably didn't want to relive it.

Fortunately for Hannah, her forty-something year old husband was a heckuva lot better trip planner than the twenty-something version. I knew she was worried, so if anything, I over-prepared. We stayed in a nice hotel in a central, easy navigable location. We planned the outings to minimize wasted travel and time. We sprung for Ubers instead of the subway and when we walked, we used GPS to pick the best routes. We spent more on dinner at a fancy steak house than I used to bring home in a week. We had ravioli at a place that looked straight out of The Sopranos. She fell in love with the cheesecake in a bakery near our hotel. She shopped in some amazing stores. No one got lost or even overwhelmed. It was just the two of us, a rarity in our parental lives. We didn't argue one time. It was the best vacation I ever remember us having, and looking back, I'd call it one of the best weeks of our marriage. Immodestly stated, I nailed it.

We went to a Broadway play. Hannah got to pick it and she selected Stephen King's Misery. Bruce Willis had the starring role and Laurie Metcalf played the crazy lady. We had good seats and thoroughly enjoyed the show. I really didn't know what to expect but it exceeded every expectation. I really wasn't ready for it to end, a feeling I never anticipated.

The morning of the race I got up early and took an Uber to the ferry terminal, then hopped on the boat that passed by the Statue of Liberty to Staten Island. From there I took a bus to the start of the race. The logistics of getting there, all of it unfamiliar, was enough to wear you out before taking the first step of the race.

Frank Sinatra's "New York, New York" serenaded the runners as we started. It was so crowded (there are over 50,000 runners) that I went almost a half mile before I could take an unimpeded stride. We came off the Verrazano-Narrows Bridge and entered Brooklyn. This ended up being the best part of the race. The course takes you through various ethnic neighborhoods, each with their own flavor. I don't remember the specifics, but I do recall how the streets didn't seem to change, but the signage and the faces changed every few blocks. It was like running through the world in just a few miles. I remember thinking I sure was a long way from my rural Alabama roots.

I can be a bit of a ham during races. Most of the time I am introverted but during competition I will greet and talk to anyone and everyone. I talked to runners.

I greeted spectators. I thanked volunteers. But mostly I gave high-fives to the thousands of kids so eager for attention from a runner. The overall atmosphere was so encouraging, so positive. And I loved it.

That lasted about 12 miles. Then my body remembered that humans are not really supposed to run very far. My right hip started bothering me. Then my left. When you run distances, you get accustomed to nagging pain. You compartmentalize and fight through it. But I wasn't even to the halfway point and I had never run more than 20 miles before. I remember thinking, "well, Mark, you paid to do this. Looks like you are going to get your money's worth. You may get to see the sun rise and set on the course."

As I continued, I was in agony. I decided to move over to the side of the course and try to stretch. All that accomplished was aggravate it worse and hinder my stride. At the next first aid tent, I peeked in with a question.

"If I stop here for help, I can still finish, right? This doesn't mean I'm done?" They reassured I could keep going if I wanted to. But the line was three-deep ahead of me. It would be a fifteen minute or so wait.

I wasn't going to wait fifteen minutes. How stiff would I be at that point? A young girl volunteer (I can apparently no longer distinguish ages - she was out of diapers but younger than me) was there and saw my dilemma. She offered to massage in some pain-relieving spray. I said, "sure".

Then I realized where I hurt. My hips.

So, there I was, on the shoulder of a New York City street, with the bottom of one leg of my shorts pulled up as high as I could manage. A girl sprayed and then rubbed this stuff into my hip. Then we re-positioned and did the other side.

"Mark, now how did you get the indecent exposure charge again?"

I was sure I would be on the news that evening, regaling the world how my pedestrian tour of New York City included the back seat of a police cruiser.

Somehow, I escaped prosecution. The spray and massage did seem to help for a few miles. I went into Queens, the third borough of the race. I was hurting but kept powering through. On the Queensboro Bridge between Queens and Manhattan, it was the only place on the course with no spectators. All you heard was the sound of footsteps. Thousands. Pitter, patter. In one of the loudest cities on the planet, the absence of noise was so eerie. It was very memorable, especially with the contrast of exiting the bridge onto Manhattan's First Avenue - a den of noise.

First Avenue is where Hannah found me. For someone who stated she was so reluctant to venture out before she arrived, she had found her confidence in the few days before the race. Somehow amidst the thousands of voices, I heard her yell my name from the sidewalk and ventured over for a quick visit. I didn't let on about the injury, later diagnosed as a grade 3 hip sprain (a ligament tear) on the right and a grade 2 (partial tear) on the left. I left her and headed through Manhattan, into the Bronx, and then later back into Manhattan where the course would finish in Central Park.

About mile 22, a guy in front of me had his leg seize up with a cramp. As he hopped onto his other leg, it cramped as well, and he went down like he had been sacked. I stumbled up behind him and asked what he would like me to do. I made a joke that they shoot horses in his condition which he didn't seem to appreciate. Not everyone gets my humor, I guess.

Me and another runner picked him up and carried him to a nearby aid station. I had a decision to make. I really needed the aid station myself. Maybe I could risk another arrest and get some relief. Or maybe they could actually evaluate me this time. But then I thought, what if they look at my hips and tell me I can't finish. I only had a few miles left. There was no way I wasn't finishing at this point. So, I exhaled, gritted my teeth and pushed forward. This was the worst part of the race for me. I was in agony.

That is when I heard the mysterious groaning noise that I didn't realize was me. Seriously, I was moaning and had no idea I was even doing it. And my eyes were leaking. I was suddenly made aware. All I could think of is to keep moving forward.

I've felt similar recently in a much different type of situation. Oddly, I do think the experience of pushing through when all you wanted was to stop aided the first few days after Hannah's passing.

Back to the race, I was really moving slow at this point and each step seemed harder than its predecessor. I don't recall how many days it took before I finally reached the mile 24 sign, but I might still be out there.

Two miles left. How many times in your life have you run two miles? Nice pep talk, huh? Dig deep and finish this. I'm just full of internet memes.

However, I did pick up the pace. I pushed harder. I completely exhausted all of my motivational techniques. It was miserable. But I kept going. With about a half mile left I was pretty much delirious with pain and exhaustion. I remember thinking this thought like it occurred yesterday. It is so funny where your brain goes in these moments.

"Mark."

"Yes, Brain."

"You are almost to the finish line. Do you know what they are going to be doing near the finish line?"

"Sweeping my body up out of the street? They have trucks that do that up here, you know."

"They are going to being taking photos," my brain explained. "And you don't want to be the picture of death on the front of the New York Times tomorrow."

So, I lifted my head. I gritted my teeth.

The photo shows the victorious runner having the time of his life in the final mile. Look at that smile.

Y'all, that's not a smile.

I finally reached the finish line. I was a marathoner. However, I felt no sense of accomplishment. All I cared about ... was that I could cease running. It was OK to walk. It was OK to rest. It was OK to stop. Anything besides run.

Hannah and I found each other. Her phone battery had died which could have been disastrous for us separated in the city, especially with me barely mobile. However, we had planned a backup meeting location. Forty-something year old husband prepared for that too.

Instead of the celebratory dinner and drinks I had envisioned, it hurt too bad for that. We caught an Uber back to the hotel. Hannah went back out for food and drinks. Surprisingly enough, she came back with that cheesecake she liked so much. She even brought some for me.

Hannah had a great trip. I love that we were able to flip what could have been a terrible day and make it a success. Today, especially now, I am really proud of that day; where what could have been another setback turned into a victory. And I am not talking about the damn race.

An old friend got married recently. His wife had passed away over the summer, a little before Hannah did. The news caught me by surprise. But the more I contemplated, it really isn't all that hard to understand.

This isn't about him. Every situation is different, and I have no way of understanding what is going on in his life. I am keenly aware of mine, however. And I am, without a doubt, still mourning heavily.

I had one woman in my life for nearly 26 years. We would have celebrated our 23rd wedding anniversary on Thanksgiving, less than two weeks away.

My last first date came in 1991. There were no cell phones, no internet. Girls' hair was high and teased and Alabama was good at football. Maybe the world isn't all that different.

But the fact remains, she is all I know.

At some juncture, there will be another first date. After all, I do like women. I like how they smile when you turn a clever phrase, how they show compassion, how they know things that I probably should know but don't; like how to season vegetables so Madison doesn't make that face and what style haircut I need to ask for. I need that in my life and I had it. Now what I get is through family and friends, which is greatly appreciated, but there isn't that constant connection. Undoubtedly, I miss it.

So, I understand my old friend's situation, perhaps better than most. Even if the timing of it seems rushed.

Some friends have told me this isn't that uncommon; that often men jump right back into a serious relationship soon after losing their wife. In my situation, that won't work for me. It wouldn't be fair to anyone involved. But as I said, every situation has its own nuances.

I talked to an attractive female, a stranger, the other day. Actual face-to-face conversation, not through a phone. Honestly, it felt odd. It was just small talk. But after years of marriage where I avoided even a potentially compromising position, it was a surreal experience. It sort of just happened organically. The timing was fine, in hindsight.

There are so many activities in my life to figure out. This is just one on the list and frankly, it isn't at the top. Someday, it may be.

My old friend's situation hits close to home, for obvious reasons, and spurred me into that line of thought.

Madison and I are doing fine. We are progressing into our new routines. People continue to help, long after the shock of the moment has passed. These people have impacted our lives. I'm now tasked with paying that forward.

So, we are adjusting. Each passing day gets a tad easier. Each experience shapes you, changes you. I am a much different person than the one Hannah knew. You don't walk out of that hospital waiting room with the news we received without it affecting every aspect of your life. It has. It continues to.

So, I understand what my old friend is thinking, even if his plan and mine aren't aligned. There is a proper time and place for everything. I just pray for the wisdom to recognize it.

Picture a young Mark, about three feet tall, little plaid, short pants flopping on the legs. A pastel Garanimal shirt struggles to stay tucked in as little hands pump air into some knockoff sneakers.

This is an Easter egg hunt and there is a golden, prize egg. The little guy hunts and searches and reviews every potential hiding spot to try to find that unique egg, the one with the special meaning. Meanwhile, dozens of eggs overflow his basket.

The boy barely even acknowledges the other eggs, only that they were not the prize.

But what if there is no prize egg? How does a child, or any of us for that matter, feel about all those other eggs in the basket?

Chasing the prize can have a cost.

These days most of us are done with Easter eggs, at least the ones not made of chocolate. We don't even have that multi-colored straw in our baskets anymore. But how many of us are out there still looking for that prize egg?

When Hannah passed away, some people told me

that there had to be a reason for her sudden departure. After all, we wouldn't be given more than we could handle, right?

But honestly, I wondered what in the world had I done to deserve this? I had lived my life in a way most would be proud of. Yet, I already had a special needs child and now we add a wife who died prematurely. But you know, what any of us deserve really has nothing to do with it.

I asked some pretty pointed questions. Like a lot of us, I'm still waiting on answers.

So, we keep looking. We look high, look low. We turn over stones that should probably be left alone. We wade into the tall grass where the snakes live. Because you tell yourself foolishly at this point, what can now happen to make you feel worse than you already do? You tempt fate; because the answers can't be the ones in plain sight.

There has to be a greater meaning, right?

So just like with the prize egg, the hunt continues. But instead of a child's egg hunt, I am searching for justification, for purpose. How did we get from there to here?

Could Hannah have left us to force Madison's increased independence? Because it is being forced and our girl is responding.

Am I supposed to be helping people by chronicling our journey through grief and recovery? Because these words seem to resonate with many people and the stories people send me are frankly the reasons the posts continue.

Is it something else, or even a topic we may never even realize?

During the hunt, I keep finding eggs. But unlike the hunts from my childhood, it isn't always so simple to find that one that really stands out. So, we keep adding to the basket.

I'm finding new purpose. People are restoring my faith in strangers with their acts. I'm not afraid of baring my soul. Somehow conversations seem easier now. Strangers become new friends.

I am beginning to try to repay some kindness debts as opportunities arise. Paying it forward, they call it.

Just like that Easter long ago, my basket isn't empty. In fact, I may even need to get a bigger one. Yes, the hunt continues and likely will for a while, but this time around I am taking time to savor the search.

We are a week away from Thanksgiving, a week away

from what would have also been a 23rd wedding anniversary. Those dates aligned this year in the cruelest of timings.

I always liked Thanksgiving. The family, the food, the time away from work. Hannah and I didn't always like lugging Madison all across the south, but we did it, often ignoring our anniversary to see both of our families. I've been thinking about those kinds of things lately. I'd really like the chance at one more anniversary day.

Next week will be hard.

I'm skipping Thanksgiving this year. There will be another one in 2018 and I will be much more prepared to deal with it. This year I am disappearing. Madison will be well taken care of with family. The last thing I want to do at this point is sit around a family gathering and think about who isn't there.

Up until this point, I have faced everything head on. But there is a time and place for discretion and this may be one. So, you folks enjoy an extra bite of turkey and think of your old pal Mark who next week is gonna try to be thankful for a regular ol' Thursday without any other meaning.

Hannah was a good Thanksgiving cook. She embraced the role early in our marriage, was good at it and thus was stuck with it. The reward for good work is often more work. As time passed, she could prepare a turkey and several sides on autopilot. It always turned out wonderful. She tried quite a few different delicacies over the years but my favorite holiday dishes she cooked were casseroles.

You may recall shortly after her funeral when someone made the hash brown casserole Hannah was known for. It was my co-favorite dish of hers and I had a really bad experience when the smell, taste and texture got to my mouth. I wasn't ready for that reminder of what had been lost.

Since that time, obviously I have progressed. I'm not perpetually sad anymore. I don't suddenly lose control of my emotions now. While I will never be the same person I was before August, I am starting to figure out the next steps for this new part of my life. Life is getting easier. This week will be another huge obstacle to overcome.

Wednesday night we took a step. Over the years of our marriage, I often volunteered Hannah to prepare a dish for our potluck work functions. She always obliged, even though she would not get to eat any of the food she prepared. This time, I volunteered myself to make something.

I decided I would make the corn casserole Hannah made each holiday. I'm not sure why I picked it. I have never made a casserole before. Boiling water can seem daunting at times. But I can read. Surely, I can follow a recipe.

She had made it so many times, she didn't need a recipe. But I sure needed one and didn't have any idea where to find it. I texted my sister Laurie, who years ago had snagged the prized recipe for the dish people raved about. She sent a photo of the well-worn recipe – and aren't those the best ones?

Madison and I spent the evening in the kitchen. We added the ingredients perfectly and made the casserole. I chopped onions for the first time since I helped Hannah do that a few years ago. It is funny how things like that flood the memories back. I don't know if it was the onions or the memories that had my eyes stirred up, but Madison took notice and gave me a hug anyway. Because that's what you do when someone's eyes get wet. Which made me want to cry for real, onions be damned.

She did more tonight than stir the ingredients; my helper.

I got everything put together and Madison made sure it was stirred perfectly. It really wasn't hard at all. Alexa coaxed Taylor Swift to sing to us while the casserole cooked, and we cleaned up.

Well, the casserole looks kind of like how it did when Hannah made it. Madison vainly grabbed a fork. I told her we would make it again, so she could have some.

The night turned into a success, regardless of how our concoction tastes. Y'all, I think Hannah would have been proud.

It is 7:34 on a Tuesday morning. The guy beside me on the street just popped open a Budweiser.

I am in New Orleans.

This is my week to disappear. Tonight, is a gateway to that process. Hannah and I often went to New Orleans. Our first trip was 23 years ago on our honeymoon. She made her final trip with me today.

I am in a hotel on Bourbon Street. Those who know can attest that I'm really not the Bourbon Street type. Hannah liked it, the festivity, the atmosphere, even a little risqué teasing on the street. We both loved the food and that really helped bond our trips here.

During our marriage, we didn't have a lot of getaways with just the two of us. But on occasion we were able to slip down for a night, eat at Acme Oyster House, listen to some music at a club and then have beignets and coffee the next morning.

I did all those things this trip as well – because I don't yet know what else to do.

Last night I ate at Acme. I sat at their oyster bar instead of a table. I watched the pros shuck oysters faster and safer than one would think possible. I had two beers. I had grilled oysters and then had fried food – a rarity for suddenly fitness-conscience Mark. It was a nice evening. I wouldn't say I was sad. I would call it reflective.

I walked down Bourbon Street. It is all torn up as they are reconstructing the pipes under the street.

My life shows rebuilding everywhere I turn.

A girl who dances for money came up and talked to me. I offered her my jacket which she thought was hilarious. I guess that's a different response than she usually gets. Well, she was under-dressed ... she should have checked the weather forecast.

Sometimes I forget to check too. It could happen to anyone.

This morning, I went to Cafe du Monde and ordered coffee and beignets. Hannah loved to go there. As my order came out, the waitress sat them on the table in front of me. I just sat there, staring. I didn't want to eat them – I wanted to share them. So, I just sat there, sipping my coffee. At that moment. I fully intended to leave them there untouched.

After a few minutes, I heard a sound coming from a
street performer. He was playing a trumpet and a
familiar tune developed.

"Amazing Grace, how sweet the sound, that saved a
wretch like me."

The trumpet stopped. He started singing. I remember
thinking it would have been impressive if he could
both trumpet and sing at the same time. But this was
good as it was. He had a nice voice. And the song
selection resonated.

I keep finding symbolism everywhere, even when it
isn't there. I suppose now I am hypersensitive to it. I
found it here.

I looked back to the table, to my past; to my future. I
picked up a beignet and powdered sugar went
everywhere covering my clothes. I just sat and
laughed. I still wanted to share, the laugh now along
with the food. But I took a bite, then another. And
another.

"I once was lost but now I'm found. Was blind but
now I see."

————————————————

Yesterday I woke up on Bourbon Street and went to

bed on the Las Vegas Strip.

There's some poetry there, albeit of the decadent variety. I wanted distractions, to keep my brain busy. It seemed like a good idea at the time. I like to go big ... marathons and what not.

But often times the best ideas fall flat once reality enters the picture. I wanted to sort of start anew. I have no trouble remembering my past, it is the uncertain future that is bogging me down. So maybe a jumpstart is in order. Fly out of the comfort zone that has been my last 25 years with Hannah.

I'm not part of a duo anymore. And it is hard.

As I walked down the strip, ducking into various casinos to get a feel for them, there were so many people there. However, I felt very alone.

Many of them were couples. That bothered me, or rather saddened me. I became sad over seeing so many couples laughing, flirting or even arguing. Then it bothered me that I was bothered. My mood sank from excited to melancholy. Then that bothered me. The brain can be so complicated.

I came to New Orleans and then Las Vegas to try to get out of my head. I guess that was easier said than done. When you have been a certain person all of your adult life, it is hard to flip a switch and be someone else. I really didn't want to change. But I already have. Now, we are just seeing where the roulette wheel stops.

I wanted to cut loose and have a good time this week. Lord knows after the past few months, that seems appropriate. I like appropriate. I like the right fit at the right time. There is a time and a place for everything. That outlook doesn't lend itself to spontaneity.

So, I was basically my same self. All that changed was the area code.

After a few hours in the casino I was already tired of them. The constant slot machine clanging, the somber faces staring into the spinning displays. It smelled like cigarettes and sadness.

I recognize both but only one bothers me.

So today I will get out. I am going to go for a run on the strip. I will run away from the sadness, both literally and figuratively. Then I am renting a car and venturing out. I want an adventure today.

Tomorrow is supposed to be just another day. That was the point of this trip after all, to make it just a regular Thursday during a vacation. But we all know it won't be.

I like to run. Most would call me a good runner. I admit I ran from tomorrow. But I couldn't outrun it. Eventually you tire, your mind acquiesces and regardless of your location you have to face whatever is in your path.

I'm not afraid to face it. I just don't really understand how to. So, we keep figuring this out.

So here we are in a casino. The cards have been dealt. They are not perfect, but you know, they still have potential. There is no folding, no "re-do" shuffling for a different hand. We're going to stay in the game, even though the rules aren't clear and there is so much uncertainty where this takes us. Charge forward.

Because that is what you are supposed to do. One might call that ... appropriate.

I can do appropriate. Dealer, I am all in.

These casinos out here didn't get so big and gaudy by losing money. I am aware of this and have spent my money elsewhere.

However, I did sit down for a few minutes at a slot machine tonight. It was bright, and fancy and I didn't know how to tell if I won or not. I felt like my granddad watching me reset his VCR clock after the power blinked.

But before I tell you that story, I need to tell you another one. Those of you who know me have probably heard this before. I like this story so over the years I've told it frequently. Feel free to sing along if you know the words.

In the early days of my marriage, Hannah and I planned a trip to see comedian Bill Engvall at the casino in Philadelphia, Mississippi. We were still living in Livingston at the time, which is only a couple of hours drive through the pines and mosquitoes from the casino.

The very first night we met, my friend Heath and I took Hannah and her friends back to our apartment and we watched comedy shows. They were funny and for fledgling comics like Heath and I, it was always good for back-and-forth banter with anyone we met. Bill Engvall – the "here's your sign" guy was one of our favorites. Keep in mind in those days our YouTube consisted of a VHS tape recorded off of a broadcast and played on a VCR. Please be kind and rewind.

But I digress.

Hannah and I saved up money to go to this comedy show at the casino. I was in my first job post-college and Hannah worked part-time as she finished her degree. Like a lot of couples starting out, we didn't have a lot in those days, so this was a big deal for us to go.

As we got to the casino, we had the buffet dinner. We finished and were waiting on the doors to open for the show to start. On a lark, I handed Hannah a $5 bill and joked, "go make us rich."

She walked over to the nearest slot machine, put in the money and on the first pull, "ding, ding, ding". And it kept going. We just looked at each other in amazement as the numbers kept spinning. When it finally stopped, she had won over $300 on a single pull. Before anything bad could happen, she cashed out. That one "make us rich" moment didn't make us rich, but it paid for the show tickets, the dinner, drinks, gas, and gave us some leftover scratch to help with ramen noodles and hot pockets. And as much as that windfall was appreciated, it also gave us one heck of a story.

Fast forward twenty or so years until tonight. I'm in Vegas trying to think about anything but Hannah. Today would have been our 23rd anniversary and frankly I held up OK. I walked through the casino tonight on the way to get a Gatorade (I know, I know, weirdo, who drinks Gatorade at a casino?). I looked over and there was a slot machine featuring "The Walking Dead." This was Hannah's favorite television show.

So, you know what is coming right?

"Go make us rich."

I put a $5 bill into the machine and pushed a button. Nothing. A loser. So, I do it again. And again.

It looks like we just confirmed what was already suspected; that I had nothing to do with any gambling luck. I had lost down to what would have been the last couple of pulls and let it ride.

Bing, bing, bing, bing. Buzzers start going off. It got loud. It was coming from my machine. I had no idea but the term "Sensational Win" was on the screen and the number following a dollar sign was increasing. I suspected this was better than setting the time on the VCR. The numbers kept increasing. I was already mentally shopping for beach houses.

I wish I could tell you it went into hundreds or even thousands of dollars and paid for this trip. It didn't. It turns out their idea of a sensational win and ours aren't aligned. But tonight, Hannah and I turned a $5 bill into $22.58.

I laughed; then thanked aloud the Walking Dead character on the screen. And just like that day in Philadelphia, we cashed out. That $22.58 won't do for me what that earlier win did for us back in the

'90s. But it gave me another story and along with it a happy ending to a day I would have just as soon skipped completely.

Today was hard. I received a lot of messages from friends checking on me today. I was on my phone more than a high school gossip during prom season. I was alone but then I really wasn't. I was sad, but I avoided tears (until I wrote this). We made it through the day I feared the most.

But the part of this story that will stick with me is that I shared another moment with Hannah on our anniversary.

Some might call it one final gift. Tonight, she made me rich. Me and my $22.58.

He wobbles in and takes the chair next to me. He has white hair and a big cup of coffee.

We are in Las Vegas at the Westgate Casino SuperBook. Video screens span your entire vision line and then some. There is wall-to-wall football. It is a sport nut's nirvana.

But our guy isn't feeling it. He sat next to me for nearly eight hours and almost every word out of his mouth was negative. We'll call him Oscar (not his real name).

"They don't have a quarterback!", he says about a top ten team. "They don't have a pass defense," he says about another one. "That whole conference is garbage," he continues. "Why don't they have this other game on?" he says while scanning the 24 video screens.

These comments continue while everyone around him seems to have a good time.

The rivalry games are going on in front of us. I watch Alabama lose to Auburn in a room where it seems I am the only person in the place pulling for the Crimson Tide. After the outcome is determined, there are so many catcalls and gestures towards the guy in the 'Bama shirt.

At that point Oscar the grouch became the second grumpiest man in the place.

Then Oscar makes another negative comment and y'all, I just can't take it anymore. I turn to him, looked him right in the eyes and say, "man, what in the world happened to make you this freaking miserable?"

He stops, looking at me like he is sizing me up. I don't know if I have hurt his feelings or just given him one more thing to gripe about.

Then he smiles. He said, "yeah, I guess I have been pretty ornery today."

Ornery is an underused word. I like that one. It reminds me of Festus from Gunsmoke.

"I'm serious," I reply. "What's your story?"

After some initial reservations, he goes into the details.

He was married. Isn't there always a woman involved?

Around thirty years ago she left for another man. He was devastated. He said he didn't want to live without her. He dove headfirst into alcohol. It consumed him as he consumed it. He lost his job. He had no one to turn to. He basically gave up, lost his purpose.

"If you think I am miserable now, you should have seen me then." he explains. All I could do is smile and nod.

"So how did you get passed it?" I ask, my tone much softer now.

He says, he's not sure he ever got over her or ever will, but he got sober. "That was the most important thing. The strongest thing I drink is coffee now. And yeah, I may not seem like it, but I do enjoy my day here. I hope I didn't bother you too much."

We conclude the conversation and I take a walk. It is my last night in Las Vegas, so I venture down the strip. I had plenty of time to think, all alone in a sea of humanity. There are couples everywhere. It seems everyone out that night was with their someone special except me … and of course, Oscar.

A few months ago, I could have been on a path to an Oscar. Sure, every situation is different, but I understand how devastation feels. Instead, I had a great support group. I bet I heard from over a thousand well-wishers. I had Madison waiting for me to make sure she got ready for school and put her supper on the table. I found purpose. Or maybe purpose found me.

When I get back to my hotel, I pull up a photo of Hannah on my phone. I didn't plan to, but I end up talking to her. I did that in the early grieving stages, but I had stopped because I grew tired of the sadness that enveloped it.

I talk about the Vegas trip, the race I ran and all the sights and sounds. I even tell her about Oscar. I spare no detail, including how he never mentally let go of his ex-wife. And how I don't want that; how I don't want to someday be auditioning for the reality remake of "Grumpy Old Men".

As a tear falls on my phone, I tell her good-bye. Again.

This week was hard but now it is over. Emotions flew around like insults during the Iron Bowl. I was sad, reflective, excited, surprised, and hopeful – among others. But like an Ebenezer Scrooge tour of the ghosts of Thanksgiving future, I may be able to sidestep a specific emotion after it appeared in my path.

After eight hours of exposure, I want no part of ornery. Thanks, Oscar.

I took my wedding photo off the wall tonight.

I'm not entirely sure why. It has hung in our kitchen since we moved here and had a similar spot in our other houses. It was such a part of the last two decades that you didn't even notice it. It was like part of the house. More like stairs. Or a chimney. Or maybe like Hannah's china that I also see but don't notice.

I walked by that photo many times every day since we moved here and barely noticed it. I sure as heck notice it these days.

It came down tonight.

The scene pictured was a happy day. Our whole lives were waiting for us. Just about everyone we cared about back then was there. We had big plans, big dreams. Some of them came true. Some were not meant to be. Others still, we elected not to pursue.

That day was over 23 years ago. So many people there that day have passed away, now including the bride. Some of the children from the wedding now have children of their own. The groom in the photo seems like someone else, maybe a character in a movie or television series and not the man who peers back in the mirror each morning. My God, where has this life I knew gone?

The life I knew has vanished and something foreign is replacing it.

One of my biggest fears initially was the uncertainty. There is still some of that to deal with but slowly, I am finding direction. I am finding clarity. The fog is lifting and there is a future out there. I didn't have this mindset a month ago. I can only clamor for this progress to continue.

It is now December. Hannah left us in August. The time in between has been scarier than any haunted house but both Madison and I have emerged from the darkness stronger. We have leaned on each other. Keep in mind for a long time no one felt this girl with autism even felt empathy, much less could aid a parent through a tragedy. She has amazed us all and it continues. To no one's surprise, we have never been closer, my helper and me.

It stuns me how our lives have changed. How people we didn't know then are such integral parts of our lives now. There is a long list of people who just appeared with their big ol' hearts and now continue to demonstrate how much they care. With so much support, a person has little choice but to stand, to walk, to run.

So much has changed since the days when I walked through the kitchen and didn't notice that wedding photo.

In many ways I still feel married. I checked the wrong box on a form a couple of weeks ago. Old habits are tough to break. I went to Vegas and had the tamest "single guy" trip in history. But I got what I needed out of it, as unorthodox as it seems even to me. We have to find what works and repeat it.

I'm bordering on happy. I feel really good about my choice of friends and how my family has refused to let me stumble.

I took that wedding photo off the wall. Maybe it is my way of checking that new box. It felt odd. Awkward. Maybe even a little wrong. But no one said this would be easy or the decisions would have obvious answers.

Now when I walk by, I notice the empty space. I notice what isn't there. And I am learning how to deal with that.

Man, Elvis is fast. He just flew by me.

One year ago, I was miles into the Memphis St. Jude's Marathon and feeling a little tired but determined. It was 26.2 miles of mental and physical challenge. I chose to put myself through this and to do this day, I am not sure why.

Today, I am so glad I did.

The lessons, the confidence gained from continuing when you'd rather stop. Moving forward when no one would blame you if you stopped. Quitting would be the easy decision. But you trained for this. I heard my Dad's words that "you can always take one more step". You can find out exactly where that breaking point is, grit your teeth and push past it. Those lessons, yes, you can see the parallels to other parts of your life.

I needed that self-affirmation. It is paying off today.

When I struggled injured to the finish line of the New

York City Marathon the year prior, I told myself that would be my first and last marathon. But the pain faded and the regrets of missing out on a healthy, joyous finish nagged at me. With Hannah's support, a year later I embarked on another 18-week training session using the experience of the first one to better prepare my body for the rigors of a marathon.

I gave up nights out with my friends because I was getting up at 4 AM on weekends to do long runs. I gave up fatty foods and desserts. I sacrificed. But looking back, I gave up a lot more, specifically family time. They made considerable sacrifices that I either wasn't aware of or didn't care about. Today, in my "enlightened" state, I see it so clearly. It bothers me, irritates me, frustrates me. As I think about it, my chin juts out and my eyes water. And there is nothing I can do to make it right.

That's the internal struggle. That sacrifice paid off helping me deal with today. But looking back I really want that time back. No one said life isn't complicated.

But if everything happens for a reason (as has been forced down my throat the past few months), then I can understand why I ran a second marathon. I didn't run particularly fast. I would likely run it faster today at my post-grieving weight. But I ran every step without walking. I didn't get injured. My last mile was as fast as my first. I finished and had that elusive sense of accomplishment that evaded me in New York City.

It gave me confidence that I could do the hard thing, to conquer uncertainty.

That uncertainty is perhaps my biggest foe today. As Hannah passed, it engulfed me like a tidal wave. Slowly, it is subsiding. I can see land now, looming off in the distance. The goal is to keep moving. After all, you can always take one more step. And whether that step is literal or symbolic, they are ever-present.

In the first few weeks after losing her I just kept moving – the direction really didn't matter. I just wanted distance from the present. But as time passes, milestones appear, and you plot your course towards them. That's where today is. Working toward checkpoints, making incremental steps. Passing rough sections in the course, the anniversary, holidays, birthdays. The finish line isn't necessarily close but at this point we aren't close to the starting line anymore either. I am finding my pace.

So, we continue to take steps, with a large support group cheering wildly. That helps more than you all will ever know. I am meeting so many interesting people on the course. Just like in the traditional marathons.

And no, unlike Memphis I haven't yet been passed by

Elvis. He could appear anytime though. And I am sure you folks, the support group will point him out.

We are going to finish this race and what a sense of accomplishment we will share.

Two bowls of Frosted Flakes rest on the kitchen table. A Find-A-Word puzzle book sits between them. A father and daughter are seated for a shared breakfast. The daughter smiles, she laughs, she sings. The father exhales. He takes a moment to assess the scene. For the first time in a long time, it feels normal.

But it isn't normal. Typically, the pre-work/school atmosphere at Casa de Etheridge is a flurry of activity. I get myself ready, then scramble to get Madison prepped for school. But on this day the bus driver texted to say we had an extra ten minutes. So, I joined in for breakfast. Instead of something quick and easy I could eat as I made lunches, I had cereal for the first time in a decade. Madison looked at me quizzically when I sat the second bowl down. I took time to join her.

It just felt right. It felt normal. We have adjusted to the new reality.

Later that evening, Madison is upset. I try all of the regular tricks and tips and nothing seems to work.

She is again sitting at the kitchen table, tears streaming down her cheeks. I sit with her trying to decode the latest outburst, hopefully before it transforms into a full meltdown. I had mentioned having spaghetti for dinner on the way home and she seemed less than impressed. So maybe she doesn't want spaghetti. I had already given her a snack, she largely ignored it, so she must not be hungry. I had given her something for pain, primarily because I had exhausted other potential causes. She isn't providing any clues and I am unsuccessful manufacturing them.

So, I ask her to help me. In my mind, I meant for her to aid my investigation of what is wrong. But our girl is literal.

She walks over to the refrigerator and retrieves the hamburger meat. She goes to the pantry and stands looking, saying "spaghetti". She is right, I do need help.

So, we boil water for spaghetti. We brown the hamburger meat. We add sauce. She helps me remember that they are supposed to be combined together. And you know what, she isn't crying any more. It seems I got the help I was looking for, just not in the expected way.

The next morning, I go for a run. I just bound out of the door and run in my neighborhood, the same six-mile route I have done hundreds of times before. As I get to the end of my road, I turn around to head back. In this most familiar of views, everything looks different. I could be lost on my own street.

The road ahead seems farther. I'm not focused on the next few steps. It seems I can see for miles.

That's where I am right now. After months of step-by-step focus, I am able to see beyond the short term. I can see past today, past tomorrow. I can envision a future. In a rare moment of clarity, I stop in my tracks. I pull my phone out and snap a photo.

Standing in the road a few hundred yards from my house, that is the epiphany spot. For months, I lacked the capacity to see past my current position, bogged down in unfamiliarity, grief, uncertainty. This morning, I see beyond the present. I see distance. I see hope for what tomorrow brings.

And just like when I asked Madison for help, this just appeared. I didn't ask for it. Heck, I didn't have the awareness to ask for this even if I wanted to. But doesn't it seem like the things you don't ask for make you the most appreciative to receive?

We are finding our normal. It just isn't where we expect to be.

Just like help with spaghetti.

I wish I had the words.

You would think after the last few months, hearing all the right and even some wrong things repeated until responding was more reaction than anything, that I would have just the words to provide some comfort.

There was a death this weekend. A young man in his early forties didn't wake up one morning. His mom was my fourth-grade teacher. He and his brother went to school with me. News like this shocks a community.

The age, the suddenness, this obviously hits close to home and brings back emotions I thought I parked aside.

When Hannah passed away, I was in a daze. I didn't want to accept it. I didn't want to think about what happens next. I had never felt hopelessness before. It stung, it ached and when I thought I was at my deepest point, I plunged deeper.

I had heard others speak of all these things before but had no context. Then it came like a shovel to the face.

At some point you hit bottom. What happens next varies by the person. There's no script that applies to everyone. But I know what helped me and it was reassurance that despite how it looked I wasn't in this alone. That when I inevitably would fall, there were open arms cradling my descent. They didn't stop the fall, but they were there to cushion it and provide a boost when I selected the right time to rise.

I was lucky, in a sense, because finding a way to care for Madison gave me a purpose. Without that purpose, I may have just laid in bed and cried, questioning God and wondering the point of this life going forward. Through clouded vision, I plodded ahead. On my worst days, she would crawl into bed next to me in the mornings asking for breakfast. And I got my sad sack of bones out of bed long enough to scramble an egg or pour cereal in a bowl.

But once I got up, something else would grab my attention and then another and soon I was moving around staying busy thinking about anything other than life's harsh reality. This continued, paired with plenty of help from friends and family, until hard got less hard. All because of that initial purpose, responsibility for someone who desperately needed me. And thus, I really needed her just as much as she needed me.

No, today is not easy. But I remember hard and this is a damn breeze in comparison.

I don't know how to apply these lessons to others'

grief. I'm not smart enough to draw those parallels. Besides, almost everyone needs something different in these moments.

But I do know how much it helped to hear from others, to be reminded that while you feel so alone, there are people out there who want so desperately to do anything they can to make hard just a tad bit easier for you. Lean on their strength. Swivel around for a purpose, even if doesn't make sense initially.

Let those around you ease whatever burden they can. Even if it is just with a kind word, a card, or one of those hugs that rattle your core.

Alone is hard. And you aren't alone. Yeah, I know, I didn't believe it either. Months later I can now see I wasn't.

I wish I had the words.

"Mrs. Amelia, haircut, Wednesday."

Dad didn't respond.

"Mrs. Amelia, haircut, Wednesday," she repeated. "Mrs. Amelia, haircut, Wednesday."

Mrs. Amelia is Madison's hair stylist. Madison likes Mrs. Amelia. Madison likes hair styling. Today is

Wednesday. You don't need to be Scooby and the Gang to put those clues together.

"I don't know, Madi. She is probably really busy today," Madison's dad replied.

Madison stopped for a second to process what her dad had said.

"Mrs. Amelia, haircut, Thursday," Madison retorted.

"Madi, she has a lot of people that want to get their hair cut," Dad explained. "She might not be able to do it so soon."

"Mrs. Amelia, haircut, Friday," Madison said without missing a beat. Her dad could see the two of them advancing this topic well into January. He decided to try to divert her attention.

"Madison, do you know how this works? People give Mrs. Amelia money when she cuts their hair. She can use that money to buy food and clothes and pay for things she wants. One day you can get a job and make money. You can use that money to buy whatever you want. Do you know what you will buy?"

"Haircut."

Of course.

Our girl has come a long way. This was pretty darn near a full-fledged conversation. Both sides communicated. She didn't just repeat what I said or echo the same phrases, as once was the case. She adjusted her responses based on the information she processed. Sure, she is still obsessed and focused on certain topics but hey, we all get like that at times.

There was a time a decade ago when someone asked me if I had one wish, what would it be?

I answered that what I really wanted was to have a conversation with my daughter.

Amidst everything that has happened since giving that answer years ago, that comment had slipped my mind. In her own way, she reminded me today.

Folks, it looks like I need something new to wish for.

He has that look in his eye of a man on a mission. He is maybe sixty years old, almost as wide as he is tall. He is walking along the department store counter past the perfumes, the jewelry and the watches. I observe to see just what had caught his eye, my interest piqued as I walk through on a mission of my own.

His gait slows as he nears his target. He sees it and bam, he pounces like a cat on a mouse.

His legs spring forward with surprising grace as he finds his prey, an unoccupied stool. He climbs up and sits contently upon it like a throne, his stubby legs swinging like a child on Santa's lap. The envy of many men in this department store near Christmas, he found a soft spot to wait while the missus does the family's gift shopping.

I used to be that guy.

But not anymore. I bought Christmas presents Saturday. Every single one of them.

I have never done this before, doing so much gift hunting. I have known Hannah since I was 19. She always did our Christmas shopping. Well, I would buy her gift – but rarely was it a surprise. She would tell me what she wanted, often she would even buy it and say it was from me. Oh, there were years I would surprise her with something but looking back, it wasn't nearly often enough.

So, Saturday I shopped for Madison, for my parents, for my sister and her family. The one person I didn't shop for was the one I was somewhat used to shopping for. That fact wasn't lost on me as I walked through the department store. I noticed the guys looking at jewelry, at purses, at women's clothing.

And I wasn't.

I didn't buy Hannah a gift this year. But I bought all the others. Shopping this time of year can be tiring. My style is more of a "club it over the head and drag it back to the cave" style of shopping as opposed to "the tiger watching the herd for the perfect victim" style. I tend to purchase. I really don't shop.

The long lines lead to frustration and make me want to try to buy all the gifts in the same store, just so I have to wait in line only once. So, I can either get my Dad some perfume or my sister a new set of lug wrenches. Neither will be particularly pleased. I hope they both grade on a curve for novice Christmas shoppers.

Since this summer I have had so many fish-out-of-water stories. I am cooking. I am buying groceries and (kind of) decorating the house. I have become quite adept at brushing tangles out of a certain head of hair. Saturday, I did Christmas shopping. I may not have done as good a job as Hannah would have (OK, change 'may not' to 'did not') but I muddled through.

I stop and chat with the "king" on his new-found throne stool. I ask if he had all of his shopping done?

"My wife is here somewhere. She has it covered," he said. "I'm much better at sitting than shopping."

I laugh. "You are a lucky man," I tell him.

"Yep, I sure am," he said. "I spotted this stool from a long way off. I was lucky to find it."

"Yes sir," I reply. "The stool. That's what I meant."

Dear Santa,

If I am not mistaken, this is the time of year where you are finalizing your lists, adding the finishing touches on who has been nice and who has been naughty. I realize this must be a tough job. There are so many kids to evaluate and it would be easy to overlook or misevaluate one. With that in mind, I want to give you some feedback on my daughter, Madison Etheridge.

This has been a difficult year for Madison. I don't know if you heard but she lost her mother suddenly in August. Her mother was her caretaker, her lifeline to the world. Without her mom, Madison has been lost at times. She has been incredibly sad. In her words, she has been "heartbroken".

So there have been a lot of tears. There have been screaming sessions. There have been meltdowns. All of those things might make you think she should be a fit for the naughty list.

You would be mistaken.

Let me tell you about the Madison you may not have seen.

When her mother passed away, one of our first conversations was to explain how her father will try his best to take care of her, that he would make a lot of mistakes, but we would find a way through this together. But he needed her help.

Madison understood. And she has flourished as a helper.

In the first month after losing her mom, she didn't mention her mom in her dad's presence. I certainly didn't ask for this or set this example. I mentioned Hannah constantly. But Madison saw my tears, saw my grief and chose on her own to keep that to herself. I didn't even realize she was doing this until one evening she let it slip. The look of terror on her face that she may have hurt me, followed by her running off crying to her room, that came as an epiphany for her dad. Yes, she was aware. And she was trying to protect me.

She continues to help in other ways. She puts her dishes in the sink. She puts clutter in the trash. She charges her own I-pad. She hops right out of bed when it is time for school. She gives the best hugs.

But most of all she found a way to manage her grief. We talk about it. We look at photos. We recite happy memories. Christmas is a time for family and you can't help but think about the person not here for this one. But Madison has been my helper. And at times she has been more than that. She has been a leader.

In that first month, to say I was distraught was like saying your workshop has a few toys. But as the weeks progressed, the uncertainty diminished, and I found my direction. Madison could have been an obstacle to that process. In those first weeks, I assumed she would be. Instead, she has embraced my fledgling attempts as a caretaker and helped wherever she can. Sure, there have been setbacks, but under the circumstances she has done an amazing job under incredibly difficult conditions. Whatever success that has occurred has been because she allowed it.

Through this process, many friends and family have stepped up to help us endure. But no one's step has spanned as far as Madison's.

Santa, please consider these words when you make your nice/naughty list decisions. And while you make your rounds, let me know if you'd like to discuss further. I've been meaning to talk to you about the deal with the Rubik's Cube back in 1980 anyway. Sorry about that.

We'll have the chocolate chip cookies and whole milk out. You don't seem like a skim milk kind of guy.

Give our love to Mrs. Claus. Hug her a little tighter this year and tell her you appreciate her. Believe me on that one.

Merry Christmas,

Madison's Dad

Today is one of those days I have worried about for months. It is a couple of days before Christmas and we are in Livingston. While we are there, we will see Hannah's family and also make a trip to the cemetery to visit her grave. Both will be difficult.

Just being in her hometown releases the memory dam and we are drowning in Hannah nostalgia. Add in our first Christmas since her passing and this is a big day. A milestone day.

I recall in the first few days after her passing, actually taking the time then to think how bad this day would be. Looking back, those days were much worse in comparison to today but like so many other topics, the unknown can be as fearful as a snake you hear rattle but can't see. Often the fear of being bit can be worse than the strike (that typically never comes).

Today is that day. And I think I am ready.

You may recall my 2017 calendar had no Thanksgiving. The day the rest of you stuffed yourself with turkey and dressing had coincided with what would have been Hannah and my 23rd wedding anniversary. As a result, I scurried far away and avoided as much of that day as I could. And that worked for me.

My worst holiday had been Halloween when the guilt over my surprise costume and it being the first occasion without her overwhelmed me.

As I pull into the cemetery, I have a Halloween flashback.

This time even though I felt prepared for the grave, I was not prepared for what greeted me.

Standing at the foot of her grave was a miniature Christmas tree. I'm not sure why exactly it resonated so with me, but my throat got tight, my eyes got wet and that weight plate that used to sit on my chest reintroduced himself. This caused my composure to take a smoke break.

As I pull up, Madison and I hop out and put our flowers on the grave. Unlike our prior trips, Madison wasn't anxious or agitated. She didn't seem to show any emotion at all. Like the other trips, I tried to initiate a conversation for her with her mom, but Madison wasn't into it today. A light rain started, and this distracted her even more and she walked back to the truck. She apparently didn't need a conversation today. Our girl has matured so much in four months.

We loaded up and headed over to Hannah's brother's place. This is a place I have been many times, but the last few have come as only a father, not as a husband. In some ways, nothing has changed. They still treat me like a son, a brother. They had Christmas presents for me and a birthday cake.

One of the things I will always remember is when I loaded up to drive home after the funeral, Hannah's brother Mike pulled me aside and reassured me, "I know everything has changed with you and Hannah, but nothing has changed between us."

Often the words that often go unspoken are the ones we need to hear.

I think about that moment frequently, how those words comforted me at a time when I was searching for anything to ease my pain. He was right. Our first Christmas with Hannah's family but without her, it wasn't easy. A lot had changed with all of us. However, in some ways nothing changed.

This is not like a divorce where often the families are

left estranged. No one wants that here. As life continues with challenges and new beginnings, more will change. But I believe some things won't. Just like today where both sides saw the other without the catalyst for our relationship.

Hannah wasn't there. We missed her casseroles, her stories and her smiles.

But what we didn't miss was a Christmas together. Unlike Thanksgiving, this day was on my 2017 calendar. It was circled, even though we were all fearful how it would go.

We all made it through, past the cemetery Christmas tree, Madison's abbreviated graveside conversation and without the link for our relationship. It wasn't an easy day. But it also wasn't the dreadful day that I had feared shortly after her passing.

Maybe there is a lesson there. Back then I was worried about a future date when my present was much more challenging. Live in the moment. The future is an unpredictable as a cemetery Christmas tree.

There was an empty chair at Christmas dinner this year.

Madison noticed.

It was Christmas Eve at my Mom's house and my sister and her family were there. We were fixing plates and Madison sat down at the dining room table. Her dad was out of ear shot still in the kitchen. She looked at the vacant chair next to her, paused, and said, "Sad."

With just her aunt, uncle and her cousins in the room, she felt safe to say that. And they acknowledged her, which we all felt was a necessary step. Her uncle slid into the empty chair next to her.

Madison has been so careful not to initiate conversations about her mom when her dad can hear her. It has been her way of protecting me. Other than a few "heartbroken" comments, she hasn't talked very much about her mom recently, even when I bring it up.

But the other night, she reached out to her family about the empty chair. There have been a lot of empty chairs these last four months. But she has found ways to persevere.

It has become increasingly evident this holiday season how difficult this time of year can be. So many people are grieving a loved one. You also have husbands and wives going through a divorce, children shuttling between parents and extended families wondering how to deal with it all.

There is also travel stress trying to allocate equal time and coordinating schedules to see everyone. Pour on a dash of gift giving, potential financial issues and it can be overwhelming emotionally and exhausting.

But Christmas obviously can bring so much joy. I sat Christmas morning at my sister and brother-in-law's house, watching their daughters and Madison see what Santa brought. Can you really beat Christmas morning with children?

They gave us a stirring Taylor Swift rendition on their new karaoke microphones. They put Legos and puzzles together. We all sat down as a family and talked.

I went back and counted, and I heard from over 30 people wishing me and Madison a Merry Christmas just yesterday alone. I don't ever remember that big a show of support before. Those words help. That support helps fill the voids, even if they can't fill the empty chair.

We made it through Christmas and it wasn't as bad as I feared. Few things are. Sure, it wasn't our greatest Christmas celebration but the bar for success this year was low. Madison had some happy moments, some giggling fits, and yeah, some of the sad stuff too.

It was a hard day. But a good day.

We don't know what the future holds for us, but I do know we knocked out another first, and first Christmas is a big one. We will push through Hannah's birthday (January 15) and then focus on toward the next challenge. One milestone at a time.

We know as we go, people have proven they will be there for us to lend whatever support we need.

We are learning how to move forward with our new life. From here forward, there will always be an empty chair. And as Madison pointed out, we all have a different way of coping with it.

I woke up angry, upset.

You often hear, it was "just a dream", like the word "just" is supposed to be comforting. It felt real. The situation certainly was. The person in it was. And so were my emotions trying to grasp the "just a dream".

Sleep has been a reluctant partner for me since that August day when everything changed. The two of us, sleep and I, have become better acquainted; but it is an uneasy friendship. Our relationship hit a rough patch tonight.

And I woke up angry, upset.

The dream was about Hannah, my late wife (that never seems correct to type). She said she had something to tell me. I apparently didn't respond as she hoped. Couples argue. But this was unresolved at her passing and it obviously lingers in the subconscious, looking for a time to pounce.

That's the thing about a sudden passing like hers, there are a bevy of issues we never got to hash out. There was always time. Always another day. Until there isn't. Maybe that's why topics pop up in the dream world, where an earthly death is not a limitation. But we didn't resolve anything last night either.

Instead, I woke up angry, upset.

Enough time has tick-tocked away so that the wounds are not as fresh. I don't feel as vulnerable emotionally as I did even a few weeks back. The holidays were a blur of activity and avoidance. I confronted what I had to, but mostly I opted not to pick fights with my mind unless it was absolutely necessary. We made it through better than I initially feared.

In some ways, I feel strong. My voice doesn't quiver. My heart, although damaged, is eager to show compassion in ways I didn't make a priority before.

My mind, sleepless nights excepted, has accepted the new reality and is looking for ways to build for a new future.

There will be another woman in my life. I know this. The one thing this episode has bashed into my head is that life is fragile, and it can be gone in a heartbeat. You set your own timetable and understand when the timing works and when it doesn't. I was told I would just know. I think I will. And I will make the right decisions.

Maybe that's the reason for the timing of this dream. There's some guilt – "perceived guilt" I'm told it is called – but it feels real enough. This is a new year. The prior year, as bad as it was, is gone forever. There is a new set of days to live one at a time. We focus on one moment, on one smile, on one dream.

Tonight, I woke up angry, upset.

In a way, waking up with this feeling isn't a bad thing. For months afterward, there was a numbness, an apathy. I cared about my paternal responsibilities and little else. Other items are creeping back into my life now. I want to cheer for a football team. I want to watch a movie, read a book. I wasn't doing those things in October. I care again. My life is returning, albeit a very different variation than the one we knew before.

I sit here in the middle of the night in my bedroom, as I did so many nights after we lost Hannah. I pound away at the keyboard, trying to make sense of this jumbled mess of thoughts. I think about the clarity gained since those early, fretful evenings. How Madison has matured. How I am a better person, a better father, and how I could be better at so many other aspects of life if given another chance.

Yes, I woke up angry, upset. But a few hours later, I am neither. That sinking feeling doesn't go away. Yes, my heart feels so heavy as it was so often over the past months. You learn how to better withstand the weight. And push forward ready to embrace life's little nuances.

It wasn't a good night. But I am awake now, ready for the day, for a new life. It was, after all, "just a dream".

Sports fans can be superstitious. I don't know how it got started but through the years we've seen people who had lucky spots, lucky socks, and people who say they refuse to watch games with you anymore because they lost a big game with you there. I have a friend who swears by a lucky rock he bought as a gag on eBay. Me, I have my own story. Isn't there always a story?

For the last few years, I happened to notice

whenever I wore a certain shirt on gameday, Alabama always won their football game. This worked whether I was at the game or watching on television. As the wins mounted, I didn't want to take any chances losing, so I always wore the "lucky" shirt on gameday. I would put the shirt on just before kickoff and after the victory, would place it back in the closet. I didn't dare wash the shirt because that might wash the luck away.

After two seasons of victories, the shirt caught some ranch dressing, a couple of grease stains and other objects of "character". Hannah would playfully pick at me about it, but I would not let her wash the lucky shirt. All luck runs out eventually and the shirt met its Waterloo in last season's National Championship game. Alabama lost on the game's final play and I ripped the shirt off and tossed it in the trash. I didn't think any more about it.

This football season started just days after her passing. Her service was actually on Labor Day Sunday, the day after Alabama played their first game this season. I remember the game being on television in front of me, but I really didn't watch. I was in a daze that continued for weeks. Football was no longer a priority.

A few weeks later, I was cleaning out our bedroom closet. Hanging in the back behind the heavy jacket that I never wear and the "Mark and Hannah

Forever" tie-dyed T-shirt from 1991 was the infamous lucky shirt – no longer lucky.

I smiled. Hannah had apparently snatched it from the trash, washed and removed the stains, and hung it back in the closet. I like to think she was going to surprise me with it this football season.

Last night, one year after my lucky shirt lost its charms, Alabama was again in a National Championship game. Down 13-0 at halftime, I went into my closet to hang up my heavy jacket. For some reason, I stuck it in the back in the closet – right next to that lucky shirt.

Again, I smiled as my eyes found it. Then pulled it out and slid it on. Alabama, of course, went on to a come-from-behind victory to claim the National Championship – in overtime at that. Lucky, huh?

I realize the events are not related. The outcome of the game was decided by the players on the field, not some random wardrobe choice over 300 miles away. But in this year where I can't explain very much about what has happened in my life, it was nice to end the college football season excited and happy; a stark contrast to how it started.

I put the shirt back in the closet. It will remain there until next fall. I won't wear it. I also won't wash any of the luck away. But the memories are still there.

And unlike the stains and the fickle football luck, those will remain forever.

"Do you want to talk to Mommy?" I asked Madison at we sat down for breakfast.

She put her phone down. She paused her video. Her eyes locked on mine. I took that as a yes.

I grabbed a photo off a nearby shelf. It was of Hannah, who was Madison's mother and my late wife. Today would have been Hannah's birthday, the first since her passing. I had mentioned the day's significance to Madison the day before. I didn't have to remind her about it today.

I asked Madison, "is there something you would like to say to your mommy?" She paused, her eyes bouncing between mine and the photograph on the table in front of her.

Her mouth opened, and I was captivated to hear her next words. They wouldn't disappoint.

"Happy Birthday to you, Happy Birthday to you, Happy Birthday to Hannah, Happy Birthday to you."

I didn't sing along. I just listened, realizing the gravity of the scene in front of me.

She smiled. Singing those words made her happy. A single teardrop fell onto the photo below. It wasn't hers.

My eyes filled. My throat narrowed. My chest sank. The roughest, toughest character you can name would have had trouble watching that scene without being affected. It wasn't scripted. It was genuine. It was one of those moments that make you feel alive.

Today is one of the days we felt might be problematic. Holidays, anniversaries, birthdays, they stir up those memories that trigger your emotions; the ones that you usually control on regular days.

After the song finished (and her father scrambled for composure), Madison and I talked to Hannah. In some ways, it still feels like we should be planning a birthday dinner. But in so many other ways we have moved on, accepting our new life without her. I don't understand the balancing act between the two. It appears I don't need to understand it. Life moves on regardless.

We talked about school, about how much help Madison has provided for her dad. About how patient and well-behaved she was while Dad monitored a work implementation all weekend.

We talked about our lives, our friends, new events. We mentioned the "Night to Shine" prom that is coming in a few weeks. Hannah always loved getting Madi ready for dances.

Madison was engaged. She was upbeat. After the emotions of her birthday song, I can't imagine how it would have gone had she been upset.

One of the first songs Madison learned as a small child was "Happy Birthday". She has performed it many times for friends and family over the years. Obviously, she sang it to her mom every year, on this date.

My birthday was last month, and the song never came up. We were busy and for whatever reason the song didn't happen. Today, with her mom's photo staring back at her, we both needed that normalcy. She didn't know how to talk to her mom, to tell her how much she misses her. I tried but I didn't know what Madi needed today. She knew.

Birthdays, she knows. She performs. She excels.

"Do you want to talk to Mommy," I had asked. She didn't just want to talk.

She wanted to sing.

Happy Birthday, Hannah.

There is a roar outside the balcony window. The wind, the surf – it is constant, beckoning, unmistakable.

It is nearing 4 AM and I haven't slept in a few hours. This Orange Beach condo is a nice getaway for me and Madison this weekend. The sights, the smells and now the sounds have flooded our memory banks. Hannah loved the beach and we came here often. This is our first overnight trip since she passed.

We were both excited about the opportunity. We love coming down here and love the idea of the beach, the relaxed atmosphere. It is the scene of so many vacation memories. Of happy times. And for the most part this has been happy as well, despite not-so-ideal weather conditions.

Madison is usually calm at the beach, but she has been irritable all weekend. Minor things that she usually works her way through bothered her. It didn't take a psychiatrist to diagnose why. We took a walk down the beach, watching waves large enough for dozens of surfers to enjoy. As water splashed on our shoes, in her own way, she confided in me.

"Heartbroken," she uttered.

Through this journey, that has been her word when she misses her mom. Obviously, we both miss Hannah this trip. I talked to Madison about all the fun times we enjoyed at the beach and how they would continue. We need to make some new memories, not to replace but to supplement. It was a difficult moment.

"Your mom loved the beach," I told her. "We had so many good times here. She would want you to keep coming here and having fun. She would want to see you smile."

She brushed away a tear and looked at me. I really wish she could tell me if that helped her or not. We walked silently back to the condo. I didn't want the walk to end because then I would have to talk, and I didn't know what else to say.

Being a parent can be, what's the word, "heartbreaking".

I dreamed about Hannah again. She said she had a note for me to read and I wouldn't like what it had to say. As I started to read it, I got upset and awoke from the dream. I went from asleep to wide awake, filled with adrenaline. I never got to read her note. I don't know what it said. I really do wish I had finished it, regardless of the content. Maybe somehow it would help, to answer a question or help our transition.

The dream is reflective of how she left us. We had more to communicate, more to work through. But it ended so abruptly. And now I just sit in the dark, listening to the waves, in a place that stirs up all these emotions.

Someone I respect sent me a message this weekend saying how proud she was of me, of how I have helped Madison with an unthinkable tragedy while also dealing with my own grief. The thing is, I'm not sure I am dealing with my own grief all that well. I have poured my attention into this struggle as a single parent of a special needs' teen and frankly, that has been all I can handle. My cup is full.

That said, I have done well adjusting for the most part. There are times, like tonight at the beach, a place where people dream of coming, where I don't feel I am doing so great. Sometimes, even when I handle the day OK, my dreams haunt me.

In my dream, Hannah wants to tell me something important she never had the opportunity to share. That both scares and intrigues me. I wish I could hit a resume button and hop right back into the dream. Then again, maybe I don't. I was managing this weekend fairly well until the dream ruined my evening.

There's so much to process during the day I guess it has spilled over into my dreams as well. There are just not enough hours in the day to deal with a broken heart.

I used to dream about coming here. I used to even dream about living here. Now, I just want the dreams to stop.

There's a man looking at me. I kind of recognize him. I kind of don't. He looks a little like my dad. The eyes, I recognize. The lines around them, not so much. The hair? It could be mine if there were more of it and had less gray.

I don't know this person staring back at me in the car's rear view mirror. I am about to back out of my driveway and the image in the mirror startles me. I feel like a dog who barks at his reflection.

Who is this man?

That's a question I keep asking myself these days. I had a future planned. Now that's wiped away. I thought I knew who I was. I am much different now. I was a husband. Now I'm not. My identity has changed and there's no clear direction of what, when, where or who is coming.

That part is scary. Even if I didn't really know the future before – which I obviously didn't – I was blissfully ignorant of my ignorance. I had a plan. Maybe it wasn't a good one, but I did have one. Now, I don't even know how to start.

Today, there is clarity though. It is clear I can't see much past today. And even if I could, I wouldn't trust my vision. So, we plod ahead slowly, methodically, soaking up life and trying to maximize opportunities.

This week has been more emotional than the one before as the trip to the beach last weekend hit me harder than I had expected. As we drove down the coastal highway, past the condo where we celebrated my fortieth birthday, past the restaurant where Hannah's brother Mike and I thought it would be funny to down the frozen drinks the girls had ordered, past the place with the funny name she playfully mispronounced, past the condo we said we would buy when we finally got that winning lottery ticket, all those memories came flooding back.

Madison felt it. Overall, our girl did well but struggled at times with all the flashbacks. I thought I had my emotions under control. Outwardly, I did. Until it finally caught up with me after dreaming of Hannah Saturday evening. Then comes the aftermath of realizing all these hopes and dreams shared as a couple will never materialize. It hurt. This is a final scoreboard tally as our time ran out. We lost.

Sure, I might still be able to do some of them, but it would be alone or with someone else. Hannah's dreams died with her on the nightmarish day back in August.

That sinks in slowly. Awareness and acceptance can be oceans apart.

It has been five months. Oh my, it seems like so much longer ago than that. So much has happened. Madison is so different, so much more mature and communicative. She has done remarkably well considering how much change and uncertainty she has endured. After so much introspection, I'd begrudgingly claim the same for myself.

Looking back there are so many things I would have like to have done before Hannah left us.

I can't help but look back in the rearview, even if that person in the corner isn't recognizable. Today's me would do things much differently, but he wasn't around back then. I keep reading that looking ahead is the direction we all need to face. I don't know where we're going. I don't know how or when we will get there or who will join us at the destination. But we're going forward.

We have to. Because when I look back there's nothing I recognize. Not even the man in the mirror.

I am cooking.

Hannah would be so surprised.

If you would have told me that losing my wife would result in less dining out and more kitchen usage, I would not have believed you. But that's where we are. I'd rather prepare the meals myself than run out for fast food. However, just because I am doing more of something doesn't necessarily mean I am doing it well. The relationship between effort (high) to results (low) is not optimum. But it is improving.

I am having some success making dishes that Madison enjoys. It appears the ones that I have originated for her as first-time trials have been more successful than attempting the ones her mom used to make. I try, but Hannah had two decades of trial and error to perfect those delicacies. I will have a hard time matching it even if I have the exact recipe, which I often don't. Besides, so many recipes evolve over time from the original, altered with personal preference and feedback.

Last night I tried to make a dish that Madison has always liked. I didn't have Hannah's recipe, so I googled one. It seemed close enough. I bought all the ingredients and gave it my best shot. I presented it before Madison and she seemed excited.

She dug in quickly. Her pace slowed from there. My shoulders slumped, and I was really disappointed.

It was fine. I liked it. But it was different than the way

her mom prepared it. I wouldn't even say it was worse – just different. Madison ate some but didn't finish her portion. As she got up from the table, I apologized to her.

"I'm sorry this wasn't as good as what Mommy made," I told her.

She stopped. Looked at me and came back and sat down. She grabbed one more bite.

"Mmmmm," she said. Smiled at me and walked away.

I love that sweet girl.

It is an emotional day.

In a few hours our princess will head out for her Night to Shine. I think back over the past year, how excited we all were this time last year when Madison celebrated her eighteenth birthday and also dressed like her version of a runway model for one of the best nights of her life.

Her mother beamed. Hannah was in her element making sure everything was as perfect as it could be for her daughter, a daughter who has missed out on so many of the events that are easy for us to take for granted. My wife stressed over this night – it wasn't easy to be the dad in this sitcom as the two of them jockeyed into the dress, found the right makeup/hair combination and the perfect color shoes she could walk in.

Hannah loved this.

Perhaps, she viewed it as a chance to make up for lost future opportunities (a homecoming dance, wedding gown shopping, etc.). We are so fortunate that this evening came before she passed so she had this night. And oh, what a night it was.

At the ball that evening, they called Madison up on stage and sang "Happy Birthday" to her. Everyone there, stopped what they were doing and sang to our girl on her eighteenth birthday. When people do nice things like that for your children, you damn sure remember it.

Thinking about this weekend is difficult for me. Tomorrow is Madison's birthday and her first without her mother. Her grandmother, my mom, is here to help her get ball-ready. Mimi scheduled an appointment with our favorite hairdresser, Mrs. Amelia (remember her?), to get Madi's hair and makeup done just perfectly. My sister and her family are also driving down and will see our princess off to the ball tonight. Yes, tonight Madison will have her own cheering section, like the diva she is.

She has been obsessing over her hair now for days.

"Straight hair."

"Curly hair".

"Straight hair."

You would have better luck guessing heads or tails. Yes ma'am, sweet Mrs. Amelia is going to have her hands full today.

These are the moments where I really miss Hannah. It is not that I need her help. Of course, it would be welcomed but others have stepped into that void. But Madi's mom really cherished these moments. Tonight, with the ball. Tomorrow, with the birthday. I know Madison is going to miss her mother for these types of big events. And as hard as we all try, that is something we can't fix.

So, we will do what we can. We will make a fuss over her. We will do things she likes. We'll have king cake for breakfast. Pizza and birthday cake for lunch. Wherever she decides to want for dinner, that's where we will go. Then at some point our support group will leave and she and I will continue to navigate our trail.

Last year the three of us had a great memory. Our world is much different now as father and daughter face life as a duo. Madi has changed so much since last year. As have I. And most of all, so have our lives. But tonight, she's our princess. With straight hair.

No, curly hair.

No, straight hair.

And her mom is somewhere, with wet eyes, looking on proudly.

Author's note: Below is the story written the year before when Hannah got Madi ready for her Night to Shine Prom on her 18th birthday:

"Do you know what tomorrow is?" Hannah asked on the morning before Madison's birthday.

"Prom," Madison answered.

"And?" asked her mom.

"Dance."

"And what else?"

"Dress".

To say Madison was focused on tonight's "Night to Shine" is like saying teenagers like texting. That really doesn't give it enough power.

Today is her birthday, her eighteenth. Many times, that would be a big deal. I mean, most folks just have one a year. Although, the more I have, the more it seems like they crop up every few months, bringing along more grey hair and additional body parts that pop (sir, was that your mustache that popped?).

But when your eighteenth birthday is an afterthought, you are probably having a pretty good day. Possibly one of those days we live the rest of our lives and think back on warmly. I sure hope this is one of those days for our girl.

I still can't believe she is eighteen.

Today I thought about how much has changed in our lives since she arrived; and how the world has changed around us.

When Madison was diagnosed with autism, she was around two years old. We had suspected something had delayed her development and thought we were prepared for whatever was coming our way. But when we heard the diagnosis, coupled with the warnings about an increased chance for her potential siblings to have the same condition, it was a difficult message. She would be our only child.

We really didn't understand much about autism; only

that she should have difficulty communicating. Your life changes with that news. The plans we had for our lives were altered. That was difficult to process. Hannah was strong and just said we would deal with the new reality. I said all the right things too. But inside, I was scared to death.

I remember leaving the doctor's office and dropping Hannah off at an appointment. Madison was in a car seat in the back. As soon as it was just the two of us, I just bawled. Then I talked to my daughter. I told her that her life was going to be special. That she might not be able to have the same experiences that others have, but that her mom and I would do everything we could to make her feel special. I still well up thinking about that day.

Tonight folks, Madison felt special.

With our girl's excitement at DEFCON5, her mom/makeup artist has her hands full tonight. They got her face painted and dress stitched up; both are anxious and in a frenzy. Dad's role in this is to play peacemaker, try not to get in the way, and go get anything not within arm's reach.

Basically, you're a Labrador. Fetch, Dad. Good boy.

It got a little testy at one moment when my daughter, who rarely speaks in sentences, said, "Hurryup Mom".

Mom was being a little too deliberate with the jewelry placement for her taste. Madison had places to be.

So, we snapped a few photos and off they went. At the Night to Shine, one "guest" can stay. Hannah is there now hanging out, hopefully with a good view of our baby – or should I say, young lady. I'm sitting at home wondering how eighteen years slipped away.

Despite the frenetic evening, I'm so happy for both of my ladies tonight. What mom doesn't want to help her daughter get ready for prom? Madison has a great dress she loves and looks beautiful. Hannah did an amazing job.

When we were sitting in that doctor's office sixteen years ago, a night like this was one of those items we felt Madison may never experience. But thanks to Tim Tebow's Foundation and lots of people who walk the walk, our daughter got to feel, oh so special on her eighteenth birthday; what a day.

And you know what else? They helped a dad keep his promise.

———————————

It is early on a Saturday morning. Madison has already had a glass of apple juice, a slice of king cake and performed a song.

Sitting at the kitchen table, she just looked over, locked eyes with her dad, and sang "Happy Birthday to Madison".

It's her birthday. And if her family has anything to say about it, it will be a good one.

Last night was special. She looked amazing in her sparkling red dress and her fancy hair and makeup.

Her hair was curly, with sections of straight hair. She was told we would do straight hair today.

She woke up, her first words spoken were not "good morning" or "Madison's birthday", it was "straight hair".

"Later," her dad retorted. Dad needs coffee at this hour.

And so, it became, "straight hair, later," on repeat. We can be a tad obsessive.

You would think she might have slept late. After all, she was the last "Shiner" on the dance floor last night.

Perched on the balcony above the dance floor, the parents watched their revelers below. Madison was with a group of "buddies" from school. At one point there were seven or eight kids around her. She would make a dance move and they would copy it. I couldn't help but break into a huge smile.

At one point a nice lady came up and said, "sir, if you will go to the door, they will call her name and you can get her."

"Thanks," I said. "But she is having such a good time. I can't bust it up. I'll wait until she's ready to go." I meant it, but also wondered if I needed to go find a sleeping bag. When we finally left, they commented that she was the last one.

I can't do a lot of things to make her life richer. But I can offer time.

Sometimes, I think about how things might be different if Madison was a buddy at this ball and not one of the invitees. How her life would be different.

It is a complex topic and I struggle with it. But last night was incredible. She had such a great time and felt so special.

Meanwhile, her grand weekend continues. There will be cake. There will be pizza. There will be frivolity. We all miss her mom today, much more than most days.

A couple of weeks back while discussing this weekend, my sister explained why it was important that she not miss Madison's birthday.

"If it had been me instead of Hannah, I know I would want y'all to come make a big deal out of my children's birthdays."

It is someone special's birthday who really needs a special day. Plus, a big deal is happening today.

Straight hair, later.

It's the day after her birthday. I'm up first, sipping coffee with a slice of leftover birthday cake. I can have cake for breakfast. I'm an adult. I can do what I want. The rain that fell all night has slowed some. There's ankle-deep water standing in places in our yard. It's a nice morning to sit and drink ... and think.

I think our girl is happy. Who really knows what is

going on inside that head of hers? However, she has shown she understands way more than she displays. Y'all, she was so excited all week anticipating her prom Friday evening, her trip to the salon, her birthday Saturday and everyone coming to see her. The people involved in those things did everything they could to make her weekend special. I wouldn't change a thing and am more grateful than I can ever articulate.

Now she and I return to our routine. And it is up to me to solo again and this morning I feel scared and alone. Am I up for this, a man who just ate cake for breakfast?

People say I am doing a great job. People say they are so impressed with how we are navigating through our new reality, pushing through our grief both individually and together. I don't remember a choice. We're both just doing the best we can each day and working towards future milestones with the recognition that plans do change, often with cruelty.

After Hannah passed, I set one of those milestones to get through mid-February with what was left of my sanity intact. Let's get past Thanksgiving, our wedding anniversary, my birthday, Christmas, Hannah's birthday and then Madison's birthday. We are there now. My wife has been gone nearly a half-year, long enough for us to morph into some form of new selves but not long enough to know very much about our life's new direction.

The uncertainty has been and continues to be a burden. I have tried to provide structure for Madison. I haven't always succeeded and when I fail, she struggles. Finding routine and structure for someone else when your internal GPS can't see much past your own windshield can be scary. So, I talk to her about things I never expected to talk to her about. I don't know what she understands and what she doesn't. But she doesn't like surprises, and no one likes it when she's upset.

We set expectations. When they change, we discuss. I've found that so much in life's relationships is about managing those expectations. I haven't always been great at that when dealing with friends and family and am still a work in progress. Sometimes, it is hard to deliver disappointing messages. We hope for best case, but we need to make people aware of worst case – or at least the most likely one. That can be challenging when dealing with someone like Madison who doesn't communicate the same way you or I do.

It helps to get this out, to share. Emotions are complicated, and we all have different coping mechanisms. Isn't it crazy how one minute you can have everything on cruise control and then the next you are pulled over with your hood up? Life gives all of us those "check engine" moments. How we deal with them define us.

If I have learned anything through the correspondence with all of you folks over the past months, it is that everyone is dealing with something. And no, all of our burdens are not the same. But they are all very real and challenging to the person experiencing them. This isn't a competition to see who has it worse than the next person. There is always someone who has it worse. And often others never know what their friend or neighbor is enduring. Sometimes everyone needs a place to take shelter from their storm – even temporarily - to locate the smiling face holding an umbrella.

Madison is awake now, beside me rocking in her chair, listening to AC/DC. Yes, AC/DC. Quiet time has passed.

And now the rain is back, harder than before.

Some mornings you just need to sit - watch it rain and think - before you get Thunderstruck.

And some mornings it is OK to have cake for breakfast.

He's flipping through an app on his phone. It has photos of single women. The purpose is to swipe to the right if you would like to meet them or swipe to the left if you would not. The women get the same option with men. If a man and a woman swipe right on each other, a communication channel opens for them to chat. From there they can exchange phone numbers, continue to chat or just move on.

This is dating in 2018.

The last time the man was trying to find a date, it was 1991 and he was a freshman in college. He didn't even swipe credit cards back then. There were no cell phones. No internet. Just lots of sheepish looks and bungled opening lines. He wasn't very good at it. He got lucky and found a girl who allowed him to think he caught her.

He has been lonely since his wife passed. He doesn't understand how to be single. He isn't ready for another relationship but being in a relationship is his comfort zone. It has been his life for a quarter century. He also has a unique situation. Not only is he a widower, he also is a caretaker for his nineteen-year-old daughter with autism.

"It will take a special person to want to walk into this world," he says to a friend.

But he's lonely. He's curious. He's wondering after being off the market for so long, what will the interest be? He's confident about many things in life. His work, his writing, his ability to eat chicken fingers, his paternal love. He is not at all confident about how to date in this strange new world.

Besides, he isn't looking for serious. But he has no idea what not-serious is supposed to look like. He just wants someone to talk to, and maybe sneak in an occasional flirt.

A single friend gave him some dating app advice. Here are some dating sites to check. These are some to be careful about and here's why. "You're clever with words," the friend reassures. "You should be good at this."

"Besides," the friend continues, "it is convenient because you can do it when you want to and then stop anytime you aren't comfortable. It's a way to ease in."

The man admits to being intrigued. He decides to build a profile. He picks photos of himself that he dislikes the least. He has no idea if a woman would like them. He is embarrassed to ask any of his female friends for help. He pens a mini-bio to go with it. It is terrible, he determines, and re-writes it a dozen times. He finally decides on one deemed less terrible and makes the profile live. Then he changes his mind, turns off the profile and puts his phone away.

He thinks, this is dating in 2018?

But a couple of weeks later, his curiosity gets the best

of him. He learns he can turn his profile on, play the left swipe/right swipe game, and then turn the profile back off so no one can contact him. He really just wants to see who is out there without engaging. He feels like a shy teenager, which incidentally, is where his life was the last time he was looking.

One night after one of his stealthy swiping sessions, he gets distracted by a text and forgets to turn his profile off. He wakes the next morning to messages. From actual females. Three of them.

"Oh my, what do I do," he thinks? He looks at the "matches". All appear normal enough. But so many questions roll through his mind. "Do I respond? Is it rude not to? Am I ready for this?

Which one do I respond to? Or do I talk to all three? What if I don't know what to say? What if they don't like me? What if they do?"

He decides he isn't ready. He puts the phone away and turns off the app.

This is dating in 2018?

It's another car ride. The two of us. We are getting used to these. She's riding shotgun these days. Me? Still driving. The back seat is now empty.

The rides are much quieter these days. There's conversation but it is mostly one-sided. The driver misses the banter.

There are things that used to remind him of his late wife. Now, those same topics, not as much. He isn't sure how to process the change. The days aren't filled with sadness anymore. They aren't filled with happiness, either. They are filled with everyday life, with all kinds of emotions flying through like bugs on the windshield. That is progress. There are days now where this new life starts to feel like an old life, familiar and solid. Others are scary reminders of how uncertain our direction is on this new path.

Madison continues to surprise us all with her improved communication and vocabulary. This was certainly hastened by her mother's departure. Ironically and unequivocally sad, no one would have been prouder of this speech development than Hannah.

I need to tell you all a story that I really, really wanted to share with Hannah.

We are in the car, headed north up Highway 43 for what seems like the 100th time this month. It's just the two of us. Madison makes a request for "buffalo chicken fingers". Her dad really isn't sure where to get quality buffalo chicken fingers, especially in the interspersed speed trap towns between Mobile and

Tuscaloosa. I asked her where to get her requested dish. To my surprise she fired back, "Dairy Queen". So, we rolled into the Dairy Queen in Jackson and ordered, "Honey Hot Glazed Chicken Strip Basket" off the menu.

Madison's dad tried to talk her out of this order, asking if she was sure she didn't want something else. I was a bit afraid of the three-letter 'H' word in the title. Our girl was adamant. The order was placed, and she got her chicken. My mouth watered as I smelled the heat coming off the chicken. We all have to learn, right?

So, she dug in. I didn't touch my drink. I figured hers might soon be gone. I was right.

She finished the first strip quickly and started on the second one. Sometimes that kind of heat sneaks up on you, a delayed reaction kind of deal. As she got about halfway through the second finger, I looked over and she was staring at me. Then she wiped her brow, exhaled heavy and uttered a word I didn't know she knew ... "Spicy!"

I laughed. It was the perfect word choice by the girl who doesn't talk.

These are the moments where I really miss Hannah. All those years we spent ordering Madison the same meals over and over again because she wouldn't tell us what she wanted and we knew she would eat the safe choice; all those times when she cried out and couldn't tell us what the issue was; all those nights we stayed up most of the night as she screamed out and we didn't understand the problem.

Those moments paved the way for ones like this. And as happy as I was to hear her perfect description, the person who I immediately wanted to share it with wasn't available. These are the moments that hurt. Not Valentine's Day. It wasn't even Christmas. It is the sharing of the successes and struggles with Madison that stop me cold.

For a long time, it was the three of us. Now, much like those familiar rides, there's just the two of us.

We share a longing to share. We share long, quiet rides. We sometimes share a drink.

You know what? Yesterday, we shared food critiques.

"Spicy!"

We are back in a funeral home. It has been almost six months between visits. The red eyes, the sniffles, the men in suits ... the scene is unmistakable.

He was a really, nice man. Really nice. He and his wife drove way up into what had to seem like the middle of nowhere to attend Hannah's memorial service. These are caring people. He didn't deserve a quick exit.

His back hurt. On a Thursday he went to the doctor to get it checked out. They ran tests. He waited. They gave him a diagnosis no one ever wants to hear.

Leukemia.

The doctor told him if they treated it aggressively, he had a strong chance. The message was hopeful.

On the following Sunday, he had a massive stroke and died. His time between the diagnosis and passing, nine days.

So here we all are, paying our respects to this man everyone liked who left us too abruptly. I brought Madison with me. I felt it would be good for her to see the receiving line from the other side. I explain this is like when her mom passed and so many people came to say how sorry they are and how she will be missed. She wore a new dress, fixed her own makeup and stared in the passenger-side mirror most of the way there.

When Hannah passed, I took some time away from work. On my first day back, I sat in the parking lot for a little bit. I didn't want to go in and face my co-workers, my friends. I knew people would be supportive. I knew they would offer sincere condolences. But even though I was composed at that moment, I feared how that interaction would affect me. I didn't want to lose control and bawl all day.

As I walked in the door, this nice man who just passed away, he was the first person I saw. He smiled warmly. He walked to me and gave me a big hug. No words were said. I immediately started crying, the valves opened.

After that moment, I was better. I got it out. With each passing person who met me that morning, the exchange was easier. In hindsight, meeting him first – or at least someone like him – was a blessing.

His memorial service ends. Madison and I wait our turn to give our regards to the grieving widow and son. I rehearse in my head what I want to say. I have it down. I don't know if his wife will even remember me. We've only met a few times and she is likely in a fog.

As we approach, I start my spiel.

"I am Mark, this is my daughter Madison. I worked with your husband."

"Oh, I remember. Your wife passed. We were talking about you this morning." She grabs her son and gets him up to speed.

The son starts talking to Madison. About how losing a parent is hard. And how you go on knowing they are watching over you and proud of you. And it gets easier as time passes. I watch Madison, she is soaking it in. She understands so much more now. His plea is impassioned, and she responds to his energy. And I am not sure if the words were as much for her as they are for him.

I understand exactly how the son felt in the moment. Through their last few days, they had been the center of the whirlwind. Everyone trying vainly to help them through their grief. Greeting Madison and I, there is an opportunity to slide out of the role of the helped and into one of the helpers. It's a port in the storm. They desperately need that respite and I recognize it immediately.

I am way off my prepared script at this point. We all are.

The next person behind me in line came up and said to them, "I can't imagine what you are going through."

I smiled, thought to myself, six months ago I might have said the same. The point is now, I can imagine. I can do more than that. I know, at least to a point. And now I have a better idea of what people need in that moment.

It isn't always words or well-wishes. It's your presence. It's a surprise call or visit. It's a hug at the right time. It's a chance to break away from grief and try to help someone else.

We walk away. I mumble aloud, "that was hard."

"That was hard," Madison says. "That was hard."

It was hard. But I am so glad we went.

He was a nice man. And I'd like to return that hug.

She asked him to go to a party. He wasn't sure how to answer.

Sure, he liked parties well enough. But he hadn't been to one in a long time, even before his wife passed away.

She said they didn't have to call it a date. They could just go together. But he knew it looked and quacked like a date.

He didn't know if he was ready. In fact, how he viewed it depended largely on his mood at the time. He still had feelings for his late wife. He likely always would. But he was also lonely. And he really liked this new lady who was giving him attention he hadn't felt in years. "Dating" attention is different than old married couple attention. And there is no doubt novelty can bring excitement.

So, after hemming and hawing a bit, he begrudgingly didn't say no. It wasn't really a yes either, but as they talked more it evolved into one. He would pick her up and take her to the party. They both knew it could be awkward. He alternated between dread and excitement. As the day got closer, he warmed to the idea. The night before he was starting to get excited.

The day of the "not-a-date" came and his nerves found him. A couple of hours before he was supposed to pick her up, she texted him. Seeing her name pop up on the text set off a physical reaction. Acid poured through his gut and he felt something he hadn't felt in years, nervous energy.

Since his wife passed, he had felt all kinds of different emotions. This was another new one and like the others, he would need to find his own way to process it.

He arrived to pick her up. He sat in her driveway for a minute, contemplating the step he was taking, the boundary he was crossing. What would people think? Was it too soon? Was he ready? Was she the right person to take this step with? The questions raced and overwhelmed him. Butterflies appeared. He remembers the words a friend gave him, "don't overthink it, just relax and try to have fun. You deserve it after what you have been through."

He took a deep breath, popped a mint and walked to her door. The doorbell sat there waiting, as if it was mocking him. He reached forward, pushed it and the new chapter began.

She greeted him with a big smile followed by a snug hug. This wasn't so bad. He liked both. There was an intensity to it, an energy. Could she be nervous too? Maybe this is all natural. Maybe his discomfort wasn't completely due to his lack of recent experience in this situation. Could her nerves actually serve to normalize how he felt? He suddenly felt calmer. He wanted to put her at ease. It was the distraction he needed.

On the way to the party she wanted to stop in a grocery store to pick up an item. As they exited the car and walked toward the Publix, he got a little bit of a weird feeling. He was about to enter a public place with someone other than his wife. What if someone saw him? What would they think? How did he feel about it?

And again, he had to think about the sage advice he was given … "don't overthink it".

It was fine. No one they knew saw them and even if

they had, it really wouldn't have mattered.

They went to the party. They made small talk. They ate, they drank, they had a good time. Someone asked them where they lived, assuming they were a couple. He followed his answer with a joke, side-stepping awkward.

They had a nice evening. He didn't huddle in the corner crying. She didn't see any warning signs and bolt away as quick as she could. He didn't answer all of his questions. But he answered a few. And he did have fun, a different kind of fun than he had experienced in a long time.

It was the best "not-a-date" he had ever been on.

The video started, and her eyes locked on the screen. There had a been a brief introduction, a stage setting. I asked if she was ready for this and both her words and her actions suggested she was.

On the screen the ushers started walking people down the aisle. Some of the faces were sort of familiar even if they were strained by 23-year-old video. Her dad pointed out various people as they appeared. Then she got the hang of this and started a play-by-play Keith Jackson would have been proud to claim.

"Younger," she said. As the bridesmaids appeared, then labeled their names.

"Mark, Pop", as her father and his father flashed on the screen. This continued throughout.

I found the wedding video sitting in a box and had it transferred from VCR to DVD. I didn't know when the right time would be to show Madison, her first time to see it. Today is March 1, her mom has been gone over six months now. It seemed as good a time as any.

The brides march music starts and everyone on the video rises blocking the view of the aisle. Eventually, you see the bride.

"Hannah," she said. "Granddaddy." She beams, then exhales. It's a memorable moment and her dad is watching her, not the screen.

"Come back," she stated, and I cringed. I thought this video may have been a big mistake.

I asked about her word choice and got a "sad" comment. She assured me she wanted to keep watching. We did. She did not cry.

She saw so many people she knew (or used to know), except they were two decades younger. She kept saying, "young." And I explained the bride in the video was only three years older than Madison is now.

The video rolled on. Her eyes never strayed. After the service completed, the video showed the families posing for photos and then some scenes from the reception.

This video put into perspective that so many people who were a big enough part of our lives to attend the wedding have passed on. It was bittersweet to see them again. There's an immediate recognition that turns your mouth corners up, followed by, 'oh, I can't believe they are gone'.

There was a moment when the bride giggled. It was a girlish laugh that I had not heard in decades. Y'all, I used to bend over backwards to create that laugh.

It dawned on me that the laugh sounded a lot like one I hear from the girl watching the video with me.

I look over and Madison is smiling. The laugh affected her too, even though we had not discussed it. She looked so happy.

At one point the video focuses on her dad. "Young man," she states. Then looks right at me and says, "old man". We don't spare feelings at our house.

The video was grainy, you can't hear many of the

voices and some of the hairstyles are incredibly unfortunate. But in 1994, two young folks got married and this video brought back all kinds of memories. It also created a really good memory for someone who wasn't there and who wouldn't be here at all if that day never occurred.

Some marriages seem perfect. Others should have never bothered with the "I do's". I guess mine was somewhere in between. But for the kids that are products of them like Madison, this was a part of her history that she had never seen. She got to see her mom at her age and her grandparents at her parent's ages. She saw great grandparents she can't see today.

It is likely Madison will never marry. Her mom isn't here to tell her the wedding story. But we do have this video. And we had tonight, our first viewing when she sat through an event that stirred all kinds of emotions and handled it like a pro. After all, she's a woman herself now. A young woman. Just ask her.

Our girl watched her parents' wedding. Despite being sad in moments, she definitely enjoyed the sights and sounds from 1994. Four years later, she made her appearance and our world was never the same.

Tonight, Madison got to see one of the happiest days of her mother's life. She got to see others who have departed. And she got to see a young fellow that she pointed out isn't quite so young anymore.

But more importantly for her as we continue our journey, Madison got to share something with her mother one more time.

"I stared at the ceiling last night, just like I remember you said," she said recalling a story written after Hannah's death.

A friend lost her husband this week.

I went back and read that story she referenced, the one where I spent the night counting the dimples on the light fixture. There's some phrasing in there that struck me ...

"Someday I will re-read this and remember. I hope there will be something to gain from it. To take stock of where my life is that point and use tonight as a comparison. I hope something positive comes out of this."

As I re-read that story, it did take me back to those dark days after Hannah passed. I was overwhelmed. Desperate. Lost.

But recalling those emotions also demonstrates how far all of us have come since that time. I still get overwhelmed. I still grasp in desperation. I don't really know where I am going. But it is all relative. Compared to those nights, things are great today.

But it doesn't take much to recall that feeling.

I am sitting at a restaurant as her news came in. This isn't a close friend. She was a high school classmate and as my gray hair reminds me, that was a long time ago. As I read the text, my expression betrays me. The dinner party sees my face and immediately realizes something is wrong. From now on, I suppose that kind of message will always stun. It will always resonate.

I don't know exactly what to do with that feeling. It isn't a club anyone wants to join but it sure has a ton of members. Last summer and fall, those people reached out to me. People who knew pain, who knew loss. People who understood.

One woman told me about leaving her abusive husband. How she knew if she left how angry he would get. About how it would have to get worse in order to get better. How he controlled her life. But she left him. And I learned about courage to do the hard thing.

A man told me about losing his wife to cancer. How all their plans were upended. About how powerful survivor's guilt can be. Now, he has moved on and has a new lady in his life. He's happy. And I learned about the courage to transition past profound grief into a new world.

A woman told me about losing her child. Part of her died with him that day and she will never, ever be the same person again. How she just wanted to curl up and stop living. But she gets up. She finds a purpose, often a different one each day. She demonstrates to others what is possible. And I learned about resilience.

Another woman told me how she almost died, a story not so dissimilar to Hannah's except this lady pulled through. She explained the mental battle that accompanied the physical fallout. There was depression. There were unanswered questions. But in the end, she told me she must believe she survived for a reason, a greater purpose. And I learned about faith, about a belief in something larger than yourself.

Now my role has changed.

Like in the story she referenced, today I think back and reflect, to find some positive out of the pain.

It's time to apply the lessons. And share them with the new club members.

The more people he talks to, the more he realizes

everyone is going through something. With scrubbed social media timelines where everything is beach vacations and cute kids' pics, it is easy to forget that a few minutes after that lovey vacation pic the couple were exchanging insults unfit for Sunday school. Or those kids who look so cute in their photos just got back from a doctor visit that scared their family to pieces.

Most of us show what we choose to. In real life, or "IRL" as the kids say, life is complicated. Life is especially confusing in the dating world where people really want to display their best image to prospective suitors.

Scrolling through dating profiles, he notices he is judgmental. This one is overweight. Another is underweight. This one has crazy eyes. Here is one whose nose is asymmetrical. This one misspelled a word in her profile. Here's one says she doesn't like people who voted a certain way. This one is, gasp, an Auburn fan.

He's trying not to be judgmental, trying not to be the kind of person he dislikes, one who gets caught up in our superficial world.

As he starts chatting online with women, he finds some are easier to converse with than others. He tries to be clever. He's a writer after all, words are his ally. If he is funny, or deep, or just not embarrassing, they may like him. But then he wonders, what image is he portraying? Because, he isn't funny or deep most of the time. He certainly embarrasses himself frequently in this fish-out-of-water life he finds himself neck deep in. Is he misleading them?

He asks a lot of questions. When he gets short responses that make him carry the conversational load, he exits assuming there is only physical interest or a lack of mental chemistry. Then he second guesses himself, wondering if he is being dismissive. In this world both parties sit in judgment of the other, weighing answers. Did they answer this question properly? What did they mean with that word choice? Why are they not answering? This is exhausting.

He doesn't have time for exhausting, IRL or otherwise.

So, he makes a command decision. Going forward, he will pursue the easy conversation, the one where it doesn't seem like work. Stop over-thinking. Just relax and be himself, not some clever online persona.

Hopefully that is enough.

He finds a lady who is fun to talk to. She's age-appropriate, talented and one of the funniest people he has ever met. He is taken aback. He is usually the funny one. This is an adjustment. Then she asks if she can ask a difficult question ... uh oh, here it comes? Is she real? Is she a man pretending? He has heard about catfishing. is she chatting him from prison or a mental hospital? His brain is buzzing. He catastrophizes.

"Are your photos recent," she asks?

"Do what? "Are my photos recent," he thinks. Whew.

Apparently, that is a big problem in the online dating world with people putting flattering photos up that are often a decade old.

"Why do you ask," he responds?

"I have been misled before," she types. "Besides, in your photos you look younger than your age."

He doesn't know whether she just offended or complemented him.

After assuring her the photos are from this decade, they decide to meet. It is a great date. They laugh. They share their stories. She has a crazy ex. She doesn't appear overwhelmed at all by his story. It goes well. They plan a second date.

She cancels the date, then cuts off contact. They never see each other again.

So much for easy. IRL, few things are.

Madi giggled uncontrollably. Ribbons flew in the wind. She had three Special Olympics ribbons pinned to her shirt and a bumble bee headband. She had a good day.

As we rode home, she was smiling so wide I asked her about her day. She just laughed harder. Sometimes you don't need words to communicate.

Our girl spent much of the day with her peer helpers. She has a great support system at Spanish Fort and that is supplemented by the Exceptional Foundation (her after school program). Madison didn't need much help from her dad Friday. Her first few years of Special Olympics featured one meltdown after another. Hannah was upbeat and always dreamed about how well Madison would do someday.

Over time Madison progressed to a point where Hannah and I didn't have to do much redirection at all between her events. We marveled at her transformation.

Friday as I waited for her turn to run, I noticed a girl about 12 years old struggling. Her parents were trying everything they could to pacify her. Dad was visibly frustrated, and Mom was trying to calm them both down.

I walked up to them. I didn't know how this would be received.

"Excuse me," I said. "I see your princess is struggling a little bit. It's OK. You are somewhere where everyone here understands. If you are able, try to relax and let her work through it. It really is OK if she screams, falls on the grass or whatever. It's OHHH-KAAAY.

"Do you see that girl right over there?"

I point to Madison.

"A few years ago, my wife and I were where you are now, trying anything and everything to keep our daughter pacified while we waited on her events, ones she really didn't care to participate in. Now, look at her. She's waiting patiently. Smiling. Today, she understands the routine. You may not realize it now, but your daughter probably is getting something out of this."

They both smiled. They seemed to relax a little. They thanked me as their daughter wailed away. I smiled at her. I wish I could tell you they all went on to have an easy day. We all know better. Their lives are really hard.

I like to think the story helped them. Every kid is

different, and their daughter may not follow Madison's path. At the very least it should give them hope. And hope is powerful. It can keep you going when the inevitable storm arrives.

Madison had a great day at Special Olympics. For me, it felt strange walking into that stadium alone. It did shake me up a bit, feeling alone in a sea of bodies, in a place where Hannah and I experienced so many memorable emotions together.

But like they have for Madison, all of these events get easier with time. We learn how to cope. Tears transform into laughs. Frustration into hope. Dread into anticipation.

Madison is laughing uncontrollably again as we drive home. You can't wipe that smile off her face. We walk in a drug store to pick up a prescription. Her ribbons flop as she walks. The pharmacist comments on her chest full of awards. Madison smiles again.

"It sure looks like y'all had a good day," the pharmacist said.

Before I could answer I hear my daughter say, "Good day!"

Six years ago, we dreaded these days. Today, Madison can't stop smiling, can't stop laughing and can't stop communicating. Yes, she's had a nightmare year, but she also made her mom's dreams come true on Friday.

Good day, indeed.

Author's Note: Below is a story from the Special Olympics the prior year that couldn't be left out of this collection of stories.

The effort is there. Running fourth in a four-person race, our little man is all smiles. Grunting, grimacing and grinning, the Special Olympian is winning over everyone who can see him. He makes it to the fifty-meter mark and throws his hands up in the air signaling victory.'

However, this race is 100 meters.

So, he keeps running. The other three athletes have finished by now. This guy keeps churning, still happy, still inspiring. He makes it to the finish line and throws his arms up again to a chorus of cheers.

Then he keeps going.

He continues around the curve and down the track. Then he motors off the track and up the hill because, well, there are snowcones up there.

This is our sixth Special Olympics. The faces change

but many of the stories remain the same. In an age of self-absorption, this is the least judgmental place you can go.

This is a place where everyone understands. Among the athletes, parents, teachers, and volunteers, for one day anyway, there are no "misfits", no "weird kids". Today is about the athletes.

Our daughter Madison has become a Special Olympics veteran. She understands the routine, the expectations and she has embraced the day. This was not always the case.

Her first few years were challenging. There is so much stimulation and a lot of waiting. If you have much experience with those with special needs, especially kids, that duo is not a recipe for a happy day. We had our bouts with meltdowns, crying and just general unhappiness. Her events were done apathetically, and we just forced her to do it because that was the expectation. But she was getting something out of it. She was developing the ability to handle these situations. And though those days were tough, it paid off a few years later as she processed the day appropriately.

As Hannah and I arrive today, Madison is already there. She is standing with a group of girls, peer helpers from her school. I see her first and give her a big hearty wave.

She sees us; then gives a subtle waist-high wave without even lifting her arm.

Y'all, our little girl had big-timed us.

That continued through the day. Hannah and I typically chaperone Madison through her events. But today, she turned away when we approached and instead hung out with the girls.

It was a teenage diva moment, wholly typical for many, but a new experience for us. We really didn't know what to do. We were "in the way" this year; solely spectators where in the past we were pulling, poking, and prodding.

She went through the day without a hitch. No meltdowns, no crying, no confusion. She waited patiently for her turn. After all, she had been through this before and was an old pro. We looked around and saw many kids who were struggling to process it all.

The scene at a Special Olympics is humbling. When you have those days, and we all have them, when you start to think the world is against you. When you feel your path to success is harder than the next person's, I encourage you to walk among the Special Olympians.

These kids are each facing something that makes the tasks you and I take for granted tougher or sometimes impossible. But like our 50, no make that 100-meter sprinter, many of them battle through it with grit and grins. You walk out feeling fortunate but also realize that there are people facing challenges that put yours in perspective.

One of the Special Olympians performed the National Anthem. He rocked it, enunciating clearly and kept on phrase throughout. When he finished, I happened to look behind me and see a pair of women embrace. Tears were flowing. Presumably, they were part of his family. Or maybe they had their own reasons for a connection.

Either way, when a non-verbal child progresses enough to publicly perform the national anthem, the chest gets tight, the eyelids get full and you wish you had tissue handy. Life is about those moments.

Madison participated in her events. She collected her medals. She smiled a lot. There were many hugs. She even got to shun her mom and dad for a few hours. Six years ago, we would never have imagined this day.

Today wasn't about winning or losing. It was about inclusion; about maturation; about making hard things less hard. And don't forget smiles, lots and lots of smiles.

It really doesn't matter if you finish fourth in a four-person race.
And do you know why?

Because there are snowcones.

She bounds up behind me like a big cat on the plains.

That first impression, she is athletic, physical looking, with long blonde hair and an easy demeanor. She flashes a cheesy grin and seems packed with energy. A friend later describes it as a presence. In the first impression competition, she wins a medal.

This is a first date. We have talked a few times after meeting on a dating site.

She makes small talk. I just kinda stare and mumble. Fortunately, she doesn't leave. By the time my charm makes it to lunch – traffic must have been heavy – she has to be wondering what happened to the clever texting guy?

I drop pizza sauce on my shirt. I should just cut my losses and go home.

I make a joke. She laughs sweetly. I make another, a funny one this time, and she really laughs. Not the polite kind, one from the belly. We start to connect. If

I read this right, there's chemistry. Her leg touches mine under the table. I think that's a good sign.

We have a laugh with the server. My date tells a story with some innuendo. I fire back another volley. I realize I am smiling.

She talks about her job. This is a lunch date and she must return to work. I grab a to-go box.

However, somehow, I dump the rest of the pizza from the pan onto the table. I pick an awesome time for the klutz to return. I hope her goodhearted ribbing is endearment.

I pay the bill. She notices how much I tip. I notice her noticing.

We walk to her car. For my life's most awkward first date, I figure what the hell and I lean in for a quick kiss. She doesn't slap me, or embarrass me, or even put up a stop sign. It turns out she likes me, despite or perhaps even because of my embrace of awkwardness.

I call it graceless. She calls it genuine. Whatever it is, my awkwardness contributes to a really interesting first date.

I like her. Before I pull away, I send her a text.

"Blown away. Had a great time.

"Can't wait to spill something on you next time."

She is looking through the photo album. This is the first thing that has calmed her in hours.

There is a blonde lady smiling in a photo.

"Hannah," she says.

She flips the photo on her I-pad. She does it quickly and confidently. It's a photo with a bunch of people. She isn't familiar with it. She stares. The man beside her points to a face in the corner.

"Hannah," she says, this time with surprise. She stares deeper. This was like finding the prize Easter egg.

It has been a rough few days. She has fought a cold. She has fought feeling alone. She has fought her emotions. She has given her dad fits.

These moments are part of the process, so we are told; good days and bad days. She went through a stretch where these moments were rare. Her dad wonders if she finally tired of hiding them, that they have been below the surface but finally bubbled up.

He thinks he knows what triggered this onset. There is a prom coming up. She needs a dress. Dad is well-suited to smoke a rack of ribs or figure out which remote control is used to bring up Netflix, but her mom would have handled the dress shopping. While her dad is handling many things exceedingly well, prom dress shopping is a stretch. He asked a friend to help. Of course, the friend agreed. After all, who turns down prom dress shopping with an autistic girl who lost her mom?

The shopping itself went fine. Madison wanted the help. Specifically, she wanted a woman's help. Her dad is perfect for opening a jar or grabbing that item off the top shelf. But for this, she needed a different skill set. And she was right. They found a dress. Actually, they found two but mean ol' dad made her decide on one, a white one with pink flowers. New shoes also maneuvered their way into the car for the ride home. The man learned this is also important and filed this knowledge away for later. The friend did her part really well. The shopping was a success. But for Madison, it was also a reminder of who isn't there.

Since that point, our girl has been struggling. Dad seemingly can't find the right combination of redirection and compassion. The things that typically work fall flat. Both father and daughter are frustrated, irritated, exhausted.

That continued Monday night. Finally, after Madison spewed out a "heartbroken" reference, her dad pulled up Facebook and together they viewed photos from her mother's page. She looked at every photo, some multiple times. After getting her fill of the photos, she looked at the timeline itself, reading the grief sentiments from her mom's friends. She then said, "sad." And started naming others from her past who have passed away. Her grandfather. Her great grandfather. There were a lot of pets. She didn't miss a single one.

At this point her dad was affected, he had done pretty well considering the past 48 hours. She's hurting. He has tried vainly to help. No one can fix this. She does understand and is grieving in her own way, the same way all of us have different approaches to find solace.

She's calm now. She's drained. It has been a long evening. He kisses her good night and they head to their separate beds.

One side of his bed is empty, just as it has been for the last eight months.

He is affected again. He feels he can't help his daughter, even though he has. He feels he can't help himself, even though he is exceeding his own expectations.

The man slips under the covers, pulls out his phone and looks at anything except those photos from earlier in the evening.

We all need different things to cope. His journey and his daughter's while similar, are not aligned.

So, he decides he will write. Hopefully, it will help.

Jennifer Lawrence is getting ready in our downstairs bedroom.

Yesterday it was Miranda Lambert. The day before, Miley Cyrus. No, there's no need to call the National Enquirer. There's no juicy gossip to pursue. Madison has decided to impersonate a new person each day.

"Miranda Lambert, Madison Etheridge, Pretty," she says all day. If she said it once, she said it 100 times. And it is not just celebrities she is impersonating. On Monday it was a girl from her class at school, complete with her signature pig tails.

The past couple weeks, our mornings have been rocky. The pre-school routines have been wrought with frustration, screaming and tears. And Madison has been upset too.

I joke but this has indeed been a challenging stretch for us. This morning, it was better. No, it was damn near perfect.

Jennifer Lawrence announced herself as she climbed out of bed. She took her shower and there was no audible crying sneaking out of the room. As the girl and her dad fixed her hair, there were no exasperated gasps, no obsessive chants – there was the absence of anything negative. Not one clue.

Since she was doing so well, I left her clothes out and told her I would finish preparing her breakfast. I had bacon and mixed fruit prepared – she had been ignoring her cereal this week. She bounded into the kitchen dressed for school with makeup on and kind of smiling. Her food was in front of her along with her pills. She attacked them all as Alexa poured out a Taylor Swift song.

Her goofy dad danced playfully with his coffee cup. This morning, she didn't ignore him like usual. She smirked. He beamed.

She has been struggling days and nights. These days my entire mood is predicated on how she is doing. It's like the days when your football team lost to your rival and it ruined your weekend. That's where I am right now except, we lose every day. To get a moment like this morning provided a high better than any drug could muster. We won today.

Who knows what tomorrow will bring? In fact, who

knows the "who" tomorrow will bring? But I liked the attitude of the young lady who just hopped on the bus for school, whoever she is calling herself at the moment. She handled the morning with grace. She laughed at her silly dad. She even sang a bar or two of "Why you got to be so mean"?

I asked her, "is Dad mean?"

"No way," she answered. "Dad, sweet."

He is. And he is happy too.

"So what color was your hair before?"

What in the name of Uptown Funk kind of a question is that? What did she mean? What color was it before? I hadn't died my hair. I hadn't let Madi give me blonde highlights or even touched up like the guy on the Just For Men box. Then her meaning hit me like a boulder on a cartoon coyote.

My expression betrayed me. Before I can answer, she clarifies with these words that sounded like they were in slow motion ... B-E-F-O-R-E T-H-E G-R-E-Y?

Oh my God, I'm the old, grey-haired guy. Next thing I'll be whittling on the porch, going to bed at dark and telling stories that never end. Where did my life go?

The woman is younger than I am and apparently her hair is still the same color as it was when she was in high school. Lucky her. Mine must not be, as I was reminded not so succinctly with her query.

Dating is a landmine. Dating at my (apparently advanced) age is something worse.

People want to impress so they pretend. So did I, looking back. Practically everyone has baggage. I got sucked in to the game and it took a while to understand the dance steps, how to have a conversation on something deeper than 70 degrees and sunny.

There was one lady, a stunning beauty that frankly I was surprised she appeared interested. We met online, just photos and a brief bio. She had done some modeling. She had done well financially in another field. She had no ex, no kids, no visible problems. We exchanged a few messages and she suggested we meet. I responded by saying I would meet her after work on Tuesday, since I had a sitter already arranged.

I overshared. Apparently, that throwaway sitter line wasn't the kind of answer that fit into her life and she disappeared. Poof.

Looking back, her departure was for the best as there

was no future with someone who wouldn't be able to handle the mention of childcare, much less navigate Madi's autism maze. But in the moment, that low on the heels of a high, it disappoints.

Another lady admitted she looked me up on Facebook, found my writing, complimented it and then bluntly told me that my situation was more than she could realistically deal with. She was almost apologetic, seemed overly empathetic. I thanked her for her honesty. Another swing and a miss. My batting average may get me sent to the minors.

Then again, in this game all you need is one base hit.

Mark's life certainly isn't for everyone. Some women might be willing to jump in and bond with Madi. Others don't have the mindset for caregiving. Some women aren't bothered by the widower stigma, where there is a comparison to the late wife's standard - done not only by the man but practically everyone who knew the late wife. For others, they want their man's focus on them alone, not share his attention while he grieves. Dating without these factors is complicated enough, especially for someone who hasn't done it in nearly thirty years.

Dating was something I kind of dreaded but there was also an excitement with the novelty of it. A curiosity followed to see how I would be perceived after such a long relationship where I didn't have any female interaction outside of Hannah. My single guy friends told me women were crazy. After talking to single female friends, I've learned men are worse.

Dating has been like so many other things in this journey. Unfamiliar territory with many mistakes but some actual incredible moments as well.

So here I sit on a date, now apparently as the ol' grey haired guy, wondering if I need to stop by a hair salon on the way home.

"My hair was brown," I answered. "I thought I still had some of the brown stuff up there. If you ask me what color my hair is, I'd say brown with shades of grey. My driver's license says my hair is brown, so it must be so."

"Well," said the lady who seemed to be getting younger with each sentence. "There's a lot of grey, not much brown ... but it works for you."

Great, I'm being patronized by a sorority girl (IRL, she actually wasn't really that much younger than me).

Through this dating scene I am learning so much. Learning about women, about relationships and about myself. Basic tenets of my life are being proven false.

I even learned my hair isn't brown.

The man sits alone at the kitchen table. A few steps out the back door, chicken pops and sizzles on the grill. In the living room, his daughter watches the same American Idol episode for the umpteenth time this week. Her roller coaster is on a downturn now, complaining of a stomach ache but also asking for every food in her growing vocabulary. She settled on chicken wings, hence the hot grill outside.

The past few days the coaster had been rising and they were riding high. She barely even fussed. Today is different. The girl and her dad are both frustrated. He has given her meds for a tummy ache. She still complains, looking to him for help. It's more of a whine than a cry and the accumulation wears on him as time passes.

So, he walks away. He takes a seat in the kitchen.

Watching over him is a photo of his late wife, his daughter's mother. She is smiling. It was a happier time. The man turns and stares at the woman in the photo. It seems she has been gone so long now.

She used to handle these moments. And yes, she struggled with them as well. It is easy to forget that caring for an autistic child requires a lot of guesswork and many of those guesses, educated or not, fall short of target. The man seems to focus on the ones she got right and the ones where he missed. It's revisionist history at its finest.

The chicken needs turning. He isn't guessing at that. There is comfort doing something familiar, something he can quickly analyze and understand the next step. If only grilling knowledge transitioned to other parts of life. Maybe, somehow it will.

But success breeds success. He wants a win. She is screaming now. He tries to console her. It is a scream of frustration, or so he diagnoses. His tone remains calm. Inside, he matches her frustration. She wants to tell him something but lacks the words.

She doesn't want to write on her notepad. She isn't interested in typing her commands on a phone or I-pad. He gets Alexa to play Taylor Swift. In his mind he knows the chicken is probably done. If the chicken is overdone and tough, she won't eat it. But he doesn't want to walk away with her in this state.

So, they walk together, through the kitchen, past her mom's photos and out to the waiting grill. He explains he needs help with the chicken. She holds the plate. She's upset, shaking and the plate is unsteady.

"We have to be really careful," the man explains. "The grill is hot and could burn us. And I don't want to drop the food or drop the plate. Can you be my helper and hold the plate still right here on the side?"

He puts the plate down. She "holds" it in place on the covered side burner. She's quiet now.

Watching, learning, helping. The food is ready, all of it. They stack the plate high.

She stops. She smiles.

Her smiles are contagious.

They carry the food back into the kitchen. Crisis averted. Normalcy has returned. Solving the world's problems one grill at a time.

The girl looks up from the table and sees her mom smiling down at her.

Sometimes we all need a little help.

I'd be lying if I said I was not a little scared. But I was excited, intrigued. Maybe curious is the most appropriate word.

I was talking to females. And I had no idea what I am supposed to do.

I was never the smooth talker. Never the guy girls

swooned over. I was with Hannah from our first date on February 22, 1991 until her last breath on August 30, 2017. That's a long time to lose whatever dating confidence I faked back in the day.

But a funny thing happened in those 26 years. I changed. The world changed. The dating scene changed. And my dating pool changed as well.

Forty-something-year-old Mark is chasing a different kind of female than the college freshman who fell for Hannah. Older, wiser, mature ... this one has a better idea what kind of partner he wants. Or thinks he does.

There were some traits from Hannah that I wanted to continue. Some of hers, frankly I wanted to avoid. This older version of me valued different characteristics. Communication skills, drive, unselfishness took a higher place in the pecking order than all those years ago. Plus, I have Madi to think about. Today, there are different standards and I'm not sure how this will go.

It's all a puzzle and I keep collecting pieces.

Unlike a divorce where the parties are sometimes left with a negative image of marriage, I was on relatively good terms with my relationship until that fateful August afternoon. There were aspects I would love a do-over with, but on the whole, I enjoyed being married.

My life wasn't empty, but it had a gaping hole. I knew relatively soon after Hannah passed that I would want another lady in my life. Certainly, within the first few months ... after the shock subsided a bit and I began to accept reality, I had the urge to go out to a bar or a wherever it is single people go to find a friend for the evening and do something meaningless.

I never did. It just didn't feel right. That has been my guiding principle throughout this ordeal. Do what seems right at the time. It hasn't always worked out. I ended up misreading a few things but on the whole, it got me through the darkest time of my life.

Still, I read stories about men who started dating within a couple of months of losing their partner. I understand it. I wanted to feel a loving touch. I wanted a hug. Most of all, I wanted to be wanted. It had been so long, after all, since anyone other than Hannah had shown any attention. It was all a novelty. The irrational fear, would anyone want me?

But there were also the difficult mental hurdles to overcome. I had planned to grow old with Hannah and now those plans were gone. There were good parts and bad parts to our marriage. We had decades of history together. Starting over seemed so overwhelming at a time when my life was already chaotic. The emotions are blended better than your favorite cocktail.

When I finally decided to meet a lady in person, it was not really planned. We had talked online and unlike other women I chatted with – this one seemed interested in more than friendship. We clicked, and I wanted more too. It was like a drug and was hard not to pursue it. In many parts of my life I was successful, confident. Not this one. This was new. I wanted that affirmation.

She was a strong communicator. We talked for hours. She was smart and successful. She invited me to her place. I said no, then went anyway.

Not knowing any better, I ended up breaking a bunch of dating rules, some I understood and several more I didn't. It was fun at a time I desperately needed it. It was a learning experience. She was a confidant who helped me progress on the journey. She was a piece of the puzzle.

One thing I was adamant about is I talked to several people in my life before I would agree to go out with anyone. I explained to my parents, my sister, my close friends, and a couple of Hannah's friends what I was doing. I called Hannah's brother Mike – they were so close – and told him as well. I didn't know how he would take it, but I felt compelled to make sure he heard this from me and not risk some mutual friend somehow playing TMZ messenger. As I told him, the line went quiet as he processed it.

It was undoubtedly hard for him to hear but he appreciated the courtesy. By the end of the conversation he was giving me dating advice. Love that guy, the closest thing to a brother I have.

She walks into her dad's bedroom saying, "Pink, Pink, Pink," and pointing to herself.

Pink is up early. It is a Saturday and her dad is hoping to sleep a little later than normal. He heard her knocking around downstairs at six. She had been up before then. It's a big day. Prom is tonight.

She's excited. Prom doesn't start until 5 PM and waiting is hard. She's bouncing around.

Backstreet Boys or something from that era (they all sound the same to me) plays on her phone. We decide to cook bacon and eggs. She lines up the bacon and places the pan carefully in the oven. She burned herself a month or so back on the hot oven. This time she is super careful. Dad brags on her precaution.

The breakfast turns out pretty good. They make a good team. There are two "happy plates". Now what? It is not even 8 AM yet. They make a grocery list. She adds four different types of soda. Dad serves as an editor. She looks at his changes like he just kept her from prom.

It is a normal weekend morning. She is not fussy. They are managing quite well on a day that will remind the both of them of who isn't here. Hannah loved these events, getting Madi dolled up and making a fuss over her.

The past few weeks have been challenging. Madison misses her mom and has become a little more vocal about it. It has been over eight months since she lost the person, she was closest to. Some days she is happy, and you would never think she suffered that kind of loss. Other days, she's inconsolable and her dad is left trying to put a puzzle together without all the pieces. Meanwhile, he has his own puzzle to deal with.

When we are fortunate, we find a piece that fits both of our puzzles. It looks like one will come by this afternoon. A friend is coming over to help Madi get ready for her big night. The dress, the makeup, the balancing act of indecision between straight hair and curly hair ... this isn't the easiest task for dad.

Her dad asked Madison if she wanted dad or the friend to help with her hair and makeup? There was no hesitation in her answer and we all know who she didn't pick. Her dad is good at a few things – he nailed breakfast, by the way - but there are serious limitations to his skills.

Madi will miss her mom while she gets ready, but she will at least have a female figure to guide and offer help. That has often been a void for her that several family and close friends have stepped into for various moments, but it continues to be an ongoing obstacle.

She craves that female interaction. I understand the need. Today, she will get it although it will no doubt seem awkward at times. I'm sure Hannah would be appreciative of someone helping her baby today.

Madi has always liked makeup. Hannah used to get so upset because Madi would slip in and apply layers to her face, wasting it and making a huge mess. Our princess is still prone to liberal application, something her dad often attacks with a warm wash rag and a scowl.

It is now mid-morning. We are waiting. We are going to get out and grab some groceries. We will stop in somewhere and get a few more beauty products. Madison must lead this shopping effort as Dad is lost in the Revlon aisle. The first time Madi and her dad walked into Ulta, the man just stood there. Madison expected him to lead her as her mom had done. He had no idea where to go. So, she took the lead and grabbed things he didn't understand or know the use for. They've both evolved a bit since then, but the man is still more than a bit uneasy with makeup application.

While most men have plenty of experience evaluating how the final product looks, they don't really understand how the sausage gets made. There's a process and we're just as lost as we would be if we were dropped in the desert without a compass or a map.

But today someone will help with this. It is a piece that should complement both of our unfinished puzzles. There's hope. There's excitement. And there's a reminder that one way or another, we are progressing.

Pink, Pink, Pink ... whatever name we pick today, let our girl have a good day.

—————————

The dress slips on easy. The hair is curled per her specifications, which isn't the easiest task. The makeup is finished, even though the red lipstick choice is an override from the pink version suggested by her stylist. She is excited, packed with nervous energy as the prom awaits.

She sits down to put on her shoes. They are new, and they sparkle in the dark. She likes them. They hear the noise, ripppp.

Ugh.

It is the zipper on the dress. This is a brand, new dress. The zipper should work. Instead, the entire zipper area separates from the dress.

Had there been just Madison and her dad there, this would have resulted in a full-on, crazy train of panic. There might have still been just a tad of it on Dad's part.

"Do you have a needle and thread?" a voice asked.

"Um, probably, somewhere," said Madison's dad. He starts to wonder just where he had seen it.

The search begins. It actually wasn't that long of a search, as frantic searches go. The repair job begins.

All the man could do is think how glad he is that it wasn't left to him to sew a zipper section back onto a dress, an hour before prom at that. About how what could have been a downright terrible start to the night was averted because someone was there to help.

Help is something the man has never been particularly comfortable asking for. It has been an adjustment for him to realize while he could probably get by without it, just getting by is hard. It is exhausting. We all need our loads lightened at times and the heavy load, well, tonight it is carried by someone else.

Figuring out the hair curling strategy, the makeup, now the zipper, all would have been more challenging for a forty-something, newly single dad than for someone with girl-mommy experience.

The dress is repaired and slipped back on. We are still on time. The girl poses for photos, as she has done for dances in prior years. We are back into our comfort zone, smiles for everyone.

She walks into the prom like she knows she is pretty. She is a bit sassy, even confident and it's a good look on the girl who faces a life laced with challenges. We don't see her this way much so moments like these, they sizzle into your memory. She walks into a group of girls and dad fades into the background. His role is pretty much done. He's basically a chauffeur at this point, a position he is comfortable with and handles with ease. He relaxes.

A Taylor Swift song plays. She smiles, and the group of girls notice, and everyone dances. The lights go down and her shoes sparkle and everyone makes a fuss. The sparkle matches her eyes. She's happy. So, her dad is too.

Tomorrow they will go back to their routine. There

will be new challenges. Summer is approaching and that means no school, another adjustment. But tonight, is about her.

They end the night. She's tired. It's a good kind of tired. The dress goes back in the closet. The dress, the zipper, it all came together perfectly.

Just like her night.

"It is hard to believe everything that has happened since that phone call," she said.

The woman sits at the kitchen table. It is just the two of them, just she and her son a few days shy of Mothers' Day. The man, trying vainly to fill the vacant role of his own daughter's mother, scurries around doing the things he has grown accustomed to doing over the last eight months; things his late wife had done; things his own mother had done.

Yes, he feels alone sometimes but he also feels supported. People stepped forward. Some of them strangers who help and then move on to their next project. Old friends reappear. New friends emerge. But through it all, there's Mom.

Often through this time, the man gets so caught up in his daughter's and his own mourning that he forgets so many others who are affected. They lost a daughter, a sister, a friend. This kind of loss hits so many people, a crippling blow that sends you to canvas.

But the woman hopped up.

She walked back into her son's life and moved from a supporting role into a lead role and despite her own tears, brought a plan and structure to get through the first few weeks which turned into months.

"You need to make things as easy as you can," the man remembers hearing. "Routine is your friend."

He needed a friend.

Those first few days were a blur of 'lessness. Sleeplessness. Hopelessness. Cannotcooklessness.

He makes mistakes. Lots of them. But eventually things settle down. Eventually he sleeps. He finds hope. He learns how to make bland food edible. He uses that early structure, tweaking it over time to fit an ever-changing life on the spectrum.

His daughter is still struggling emotionally with the loss of her mom. However, in other areas of her life she is thriving. She isn't the same girl she was last August. She's more independent, more communicative, more engaged and dare we say, more social? There's hope for her to someday have a job and a life her parents used to doubt she would ever have.

Mom commends her son for her granddaughter's progress. The results are there, despite his struggles. He appreciates the sentiment. He appreciates the help she continues to provide. His kitchen hasn't been cleaner. His laundry is caught up. His daughter has new dresses. These are things her son tries and while he has improved, he's a rank amateur. Mom swoops in to do what she can.

He doesn't know how to ever thank her enough.

Sunday is Mothers' Day and like many of these recent occasions, it will be difficult.

Later that evening, the man sits down to write. This has been his normal outlet when he gets a moment to himself. This is his routine, his friend.

Just like she said to do.

A tear slides down his cheek. He thinks about that night of unthinkable phone calls. He thinks about life since that awful moment and all the people who rushed in. How their lives are different now. Then, he thinks about Mothers' Day and about the lady who sat in his kitchen earlier that day.

The man doesn't need as much help as he once did.

But he knows that help is there should he need it. A mother's job is to teach her child how to survive on their own.

Sounds like Mom did a really good job.

She kept saying, "so sad". Over and over again.

You don't need a lot of words when you have the right ones.

They stand a few feet from her mother's headstone. It's her first Mothers' Day without her mom.

We're not sure what she understands. Does she wonder why her dad drags her out to this field to look at a rock with her mother's name on it? Is she confused why they talk to her mom in a cemetery today instead of looking at a photo as they do other times?

She looks to her dad for guidance. He looks around hoping for someone to guide him. They are the only people there sweating. Words fail him, so he just gives her another hug. If hugs had a cost, he would be in debt. They discuss her eventful May; her prom, her graduation ceremony and the transition to summer.

They tell her mom how her family made Madison

smile the night before. Her uncle is remodeling an old house and turning it into a camp. He's mid-project but it was a great spot to decorate for a surprise graduation party. Our girl will go through the high school graduation ceremony Tuesday. She'll continue to attend school until she is 21 but she will walk with her classmates. She's getting excited about it, so the party stoked her fervor.

At the party, there are signs, banners and various festive items greeting her as she arrives. There are oysters and a shrimp boil awaiting. She keeps reading the signs saying congratulations on your graduation. When she says the two words, they are almost indistinguishable. She says them a lot.

Her mom would have loved the party. Surrounded by family with the men doing the cooking … it was her kind of scene. At one-point Madison mentions her mom's name. Her dad tells a story about her mother. It breaks the ice. More are told. The girl cracks a smile. This is a hard weekend, and everyone here knows that all too well.

But in this year packed with memories, good and otherwise, another was made at her graduation party. It was a sweet gesture for a young woman who is struggling to find her way in her new life.

Yes, she is sad. Yes, she often asks for guidance from a man who has more questions than answers. And yes, she is enduring a Mothers' Day without her mom.

One of her dad's Mothers' Day memories came many years ago when Madison was younger. She was obsessed with McDonald's caramel sundaes and repeated the phrase over and again. She stayed with her father while her mom got some alone time, a rare occurrence for Hannah in those days. We all need a break sometimes.

It didn't go particularly well for her dad with meltdowns and frustration. Since her father didn't want to bother her mother today, he tried his best. He used all his tricks. Finally, after hours of unhappiness, her mother called to check on things and heard the girl screaming in the background.

"Just take her to get a caramel sundae," she said.

Off they went and things magically improved. It was simple advice that for some reason her dad didn't consider.

As they left the cemetery Sunday, they rode without speaking. A Gary Allan song played, Hannah always liked his music. And the man had a thought.

A few minutes later he pulled into McDonald's.

"Two caramel sundaes, please."

And with that memory, with that order, "so sad", takes a break. We all need a break sometimes.

Our girl did well tonight. She went through the graduation ceremony. She went first.

First.

Yes, the girl who learns by watching. Yes, the girl who isn't trusted to cross the street unaccompanied. Yes, the same girl who rarely took a step beyond school or home outside of her mother's shadow for 18 years.

That girl went first tonight, alone, with no one to model after. And she did it smiling.

No meltdown. No escape toward the end zone. No plop down in the grass wailing. Her ten-year-old self would have been astounded.

She matured. She handled the moment. She made us

all proud.

As the scene unfolded, it was difficult for those who knew her backstory to avoid thinking about the person most responsible for laying the foundation for this moment. The person who was there every day, taking her to school, dropping everything to pick her up early when she had behavior issues, getting her after school and being her biggest advocate, that person was absent from the fun post-graduation photo op.

It was like Hannah got to be on the team through all of the practices but never got to go to the game. And there was at least one man in the stadium that struggled with that notion.

About ten minutes before the graduation service commenced, a lump appeared in that man's throat. His daughter lost her mother about two weeks into her senior year. There were impossible moments. There were some triumphs. Then there were setbacks and then the whole scenario would repeat. But tonight, she flourished.

They went for a pizza party after graduation. Madison enjoyed being the center of attention. She helped the waiter bus the table. After they headed back home, she got ready for bed.

Her dad tucked her in and walked away. As he flipped

off her light switch, something stopped him, and he retraced his steps back to her bed. He gave her a peck on the cheek and told her how well she did tonight and also how proud he is of her.

She continues to grow her vocabulary. Sometimes, she's like that boy on a date trying to impress with words he doesn't really use correctly. Other times, she can be downright poetic.

She said one word.

It stopped her father. He searched for context.

They had talked months ago about being brave when things were hard. How sometimes life doesn't seem fair but tough people keep trying, keep pushing ahead. He told her it was OK to be sad. It was OK to cry. But it was not OK to let it make her behave badly or not do the things she knew how to do. When she wanted to lose control, she needed to be ... and he used that word she surprised him with tonight.

Her father talks to her a lot but as most of you know, as both a man and a dad, he has little chance of effectively communicating with a nineteen-year-old female. Add in her unique situation and her father has little absolute understanding of what she comprehends, recalls or can utilize. But she continues to show glimpses of understanding. Tonight, was more than a glimpse though.

This week she handled a visit to her mom's grave on Mother's Day. Two days later, she walked across that field on graduation night. She didn't flinch. Either time.

Maybe her dad is biased but it seems she picked the perfect word.

"Strong."

We sit in a doctor's office waiting room. We wait. We try to entertain ourselves. Patience is not a strength for our girl and it is just as much due to genetics as her autism.

She blurts out a nonsense phrase. It is loud, and the crowd of bored people start to stare.

Her dad tries to quiet her, to calm her. She's bored. She's impatient. She's unsure of exactly what the doctor is going to try to do. She blurts out another phrase. "Coke Zero. Straight Hair."

Her dad locks eyes with a man a few chairs over. He has kind eyes. He smiles. He starts to speak in our direction and explains he is 90 years old. So is his wife, seated beside him. She gets up and wobbles over to the desk to grab a form. He asks her if she needs any help. She smiles and starts to fill out the form.

He starts to talk to our girl. She ignores him, but he doesn't seem to notice.

He says he and his wife have been married for 65 years. He drove them to the appointment. They both have cancer, but they are, "doing great for 90". He talks about World War II and how Tom Brokaw (he called him Broke-off) interviewed him about his experience in Hiroshima and Nagasaki.

Our girl's dad is smiling. He thinks about his own grandfather who also served in World War II, was married over 60 years and mispronounced more names than Yogi Berra.

A 65-year marriage is a marvel. Most of us will never spend that much time with anyone. Our girl's parents were together for over 25, married for 22 and her dad doesn't remember what life was like before then. Some couples are destined for longevity. Others face a different plan.

The woman returns the form and slides in beside her groom. He asked her if she needs anything. What exactly is he is going to get her in a doctor's office waiting room? I suspect this is more out of habit and affection than anything. They are sweet together and so very likable. Madison's dad catches himself smiling again.

Our girl blurts out another phrase. "Martina McBride. School tomorrow."

The older man looks back over, this time with a knowing look. As Madison becomes more agitated, her dad responds with calm. She goes up, he goes down. Some moments make this tactic easier than others.

Everyone doesn't always understand when our girl lets her autism show. It is a waiting room. There is a captive audience so every conversation, every behavior is scrutinized. She starts to stand. She wants to dart across the room. Her dad intercepts her, and they slowly walk across the room.

As they walk back, the older man rises and steps forward.

"Can I get y'all anything?"

"Thank you, sir, but we will be fine. Just a little anxious waiting."

"You are doing a good job. I'm proud of you. Proud of you both."

Madison and her escort stop. Her dad didn't expect those words, especially from a stranger inserting himself into a situation most can't run away fast enough from.

"We are trying our best. Thank you for that."

Madison is sitting now. Her father feels newfound support. May hasn't been easy, the past two weeks especially. Few know or understand. Sometimes words cut deep, filling your chest with warmth. This is real.

Madison's name gets called and she hops up darting for the open door.

Her dad looks over at their new friend.

"You take care of yourself. That was really nice of you earlier. It's the little things that matter sometimes. We appreciate it."

"Ahh, I didn't do anything. It doesn't cost a nickel to be nice."

Sometimes you come to see the doctor for one problem and instead get treated for something you needed more.

And unlike the doctor's visit, this didn't cost a nickel.

I walk into the stadium. In a way it is like coming home.

So much has changed since I last occupied this space. I am older, wiser. I am now a widower, a single dad.

Every year since 1999, I've walked through this gate. If you want to think about it, that was a lifetime ago. But honestly, so was last year.

The last time I walked down this concourse, I was married, sheltered, oblivious. Now, I feel like none of those things and see the world differently.

Someone I know is ahead. I walk up and speak. It catches the man by surprise and the other man's eyes betray his thoughts. You can see the moment he recalls, "oh, Mark's wife."

I see panic in his eyes. Then they shift, now they are sad eyes. It seems I collect those like baseball cards.

Most don't mention it directly. They use code.

"How are you," and they emphasize the 'you'.

This is a tough topic, and many don't know how to broach it with someone that they don't know well.

So, how am I?

I ask myself that same question periodically.

Most of the time I am fine. I am still grieving. I am not depressed. Life is harder now, but I am stronger, more capable, more confident. You don't come out of something like this as the same person. But there are moments when that strength disappears.

The other evening Madi crawled into bed beside me and we watched TV. After a few minutes I absentmindedly thought, Hannah will be home soon.

I knew better, but my brain played a trick on me. It has been over nine months since she left us. I know she isn't coming home. But those moments persist. I suspect they will continue for a while.

Do you want to know the hardest part? It's not the holidays, the birthdays or even the solitude with Madison.

The hardest part is when something happens that there's really just one other person who ever lived who would truly appreciate the moment, and that one person is gone. Our shared history is now a solo act. Something happens with a mutual friend or a restaurant we liked or a television show we "discovered", those are the moments that strike me.

But mainly it is something with Madison where she demonstrates how much she has progressed.

Mother's Day stirred things up. Graduation piled on.

Madison is doing so well. She sent me an unsolicited text the other day saying she misses her mom. Those are the moments we would really love to share with Hannah and it is a gut-punch to miss out on that.

I'm not only grieving the loss of a wife, but also that shared history. It feels like I am starting over. There are weeks that go by where things seem easy. Other times the weight on my chest returns, like a house guest that drinks all the juice and raids the pantry for snacks. In a way it is familiar, so you tolerate its presence but sure wish it would behave while it's visiting.

So, I was in the baseball stadium last week. I got one day to go try to be "normal".

It rained.

That is the difference between this year and last year ... the perspective to appreciate the opportunity as opposed to the end result.

We move on. We grieve. We heal. Time passes and the things that use to cause a big lump in your throat cause a smaller one instead. That's progress.

So, how am I?

Tonight, I am good. I mowed the lawn. I grilled and

had a beer. Madison is content. I had time to write.

Things I once took for granted are noticed. I remember to be happy.

The grief is still there. You just learn how to walk alongside it.

Even when it rains.

Your brain is like a big city. There are some parts of it you best not visit after dark.

"If we were vampires and death was a joke
We'd go out on the sidewalk and smoke
And laugh at all the lovers and their plans
I wouldn't feel the need to hold your hand"

I'm listening to Jason Isbell again. It's late and I know better.

I think back on today. On the last week. On the last month. Hell, on the last life.

Her jewelry sits in a box on the table. I got it out to do something for Madison. Our girl has had a rough week and I wondered if there was something that might help. Sifting through that is like a visit from the ghost of gifts past.

The box is now put away, but the memories didn't go with it.

My hand shakes as I type. Isbell croons.

"Maybe time running out is a gift
I'll work hard 'til the end of my shift
And give you every second I can find
And hope it isn't me who's left behind"

It was me left behind. No one knows the who, the when or the why. That is one more thing we can't control. I sometimes think how things would have been had I been the one who left. How would Hannah and Madison be progressing? And then that drifts into how would Hannah feel about our new lives?

Of course, she would want us to search for happiness. She would want us to find ways to make our lives easier. She would want us to remember the happy times. We are doing all of those things.

I feel so different. Lost but found. Scattered but focused. This new life as a single caretaker of an autistic young adult has stretched my patience. This new life as a widower has caused me to retroactively face problems with my marriage. This new life as a single person has shown me that I have really never been alone before. All are challenging adjustments.

Some days are a struggle. Some nights are worse than that.

But other times we flourish. We smile. We share. We connect.

It is summer now. By the time summer ends, she will have been gone a year. Memories fade, as do regrets. That ol' saying, "time heals all wounds" ... well, we are working on that.

"It's knowing that this can't go on forever
Likely one of us will have to spend some days alone
Maybe we'll get forty years together
But one day I'll be gone
Or one day you'll be gone"

The song is nearly finished. My fingers type away, now as steady as they come. I like the song. It resonates.

I look around this brain I'm visiting. This place doesn't look so rough after all.

Author's note: After Hannah's passing, many new people entered our lives. One of them told this story and I felt compelled to record it.

If only she had tried harder. She knows such thinking won't help. It won't bring anyone back. It certainly won't make her feel any better. Yet, it persists.

They had bonded a few weeks ago. The lady, we will call her Cricket, recognized parts of herself in this young lady wandering through the fog hoping for a new direction.

Tonight, she's crying, and tears don't come easy for her. Cricket spent a lifetime building walls to keep from feeling, well, anything that touches her soul. There's been a void she has only partially filled to this point.

Cricket has been sober twelve years. Twelve years is a lifetime for a recovering addict. Her vice was alcohol, a way to numb the pain of a tragic back story. Her ex-husband was also an addict, but he fell farther. She escaped, overcame, flourished. Hers is a success story.

Cricket isn't feeling like a success tonight. She reflects on her own journey. One day sober, then one week, one month, one year. She got the medallion from Alcoholics Anonymous. Each year as that medallion comes her way on her sobriety date, something she looks forward to all year, she does something that may strike people as odd.

She gives it away.

She finds someone who needs hope. She gives them her story. Some get the personalized version. She ministers to addicts. She's been there. This isn't evangelizing on hypotheticals. What worked for her – an abundance of faith, willpower and maternal love – may not be the path for everyone but she is testimony that there is a way out. She's articulate, beautiful, genuine – all ways likable - which helps with connecting.

She met Nikki earlier in the month at one of her meetings. Cricket gave testimony and then reached out afterward. She recognized the signs. She was worried where Nikki would go but the fact that she dared step into a church was a great first step.

They spoke at length. Cricket could see parallels from her own struggle. A young mother on a path to destruction.

Nikki left that night with a vision for hope and Cricket's twelve-year medallion.

I always try to find someone who really needs it, she explains. She needs to see there is a future for her and her children.

Cricket worried about her all week. Would she return for the next meeting or was this a one-time Hail Mary?

It turns out Nikki did show. And sought out her new friend, a role model (Cricket scoffs at the term).

But that was their only reunion.

If this was a movie, we'd talk about how that one night with Cricket was the turning point for Nikki. How she took that gifted medallion as motivation to earn her own. And perhaps awarded to someone else one day in a neatly wrapped up pay-it-forward plotline.

Real life, unfortunately, features far more stories like Nikki's than Cricket's.

Nikki lost her battle last night. And the world lost Nikki. And Cricket is left wondering how she could have done more, done something different, something to improve her odds. She understands this is a peril of her work. She can't save everyone. People must move towards salvation if they seek it.

The next morning comes quickly. Cricket feels hungover. Oh, the irony. She can't shake the images in her head.

Yet, her strength will allow her to overcome. She will persevere. She will be back next week, waiting to help the next Nikki.

Her mission has life or death consequences. She received a harsh reminder, as if she could ever forget. This moment will drive her. Focus her. And remind her how far she has traveled in her own battle.

I was mid-twenties and had my own money for the first time in my life. Looking back, it wasn't really very much money, but it was a lot in comparison to my days of hot pockets and Chek colas. I wanted to do something nice for someone. I wanted to share. So, I booked a trip.

Growing up I always loved sports. As far back as I can recall, there was a ball of some kind within reach and the only television programs I really cared about had a scoreboard in the corner. My dad and I watched a lot of sports together. We watched football on fall weekends, basketball during the winter and baseball all spring and summer. We would watch the Cubs during the day - their ballpark Wrigley Field didn't have lights in those days – and we would watch the Braves at night.

When I was able, I went to Atlanta and saw the Braves play in person. Atlanta wasn't that far away so that was an easy trip. I followed that with a trip to Chicago to see the Cubs. I flew up by myself one morning, took the train to the park, bought a scalped ticket for $20 and basically walked around the ballpark for three hours. I then meandered through

Wrigleyville outside the park until it was time to head back to the airport for a flight. For some reason, young Mark didn't think an overnight trip was necessary. If I tried that today, I might need to sleep for a week.

I decided my dad needed to see Wrigley. I put the plans in motion and bought everything, non-refundable. I figured he wouldn't let me waste the tickets, so he would have to go. Again, not exactly thought through. I sprung the idea on him as an idea. He thought, "yeah, that would be fun."

"Good," I answered. "Because we are going this summer."

He stuttered and stammered and tried to make excuses why he couldn't go. Then, he relented. He knew it would potentially be a trip we would always remember. He was right.

We flew up early one morning and took the train to the hotel, dropped off our bags and headed to Wrigley. The Cubs were playing the Mets – I don't remember who won – but we did have a good time. Dad bought a floppy bucket hat with the Cubs' "C" on it. I remember it was hot. After the game we walked around Wrigleyville and then headed back to the hotel. We were staying on Michigan Avenue which was a tad bit different than rural Alabama.

First, all the roads were paved. Just about everyone wore shoes and sleeves. Almost no one spoke as you met them on the street. We couldn't get sweet tea, or grits and people looked at us funny when Dad asked, would you like a coke? And I answered, what kind? ... then handed him a Dr. Pepper.

We ate food from a street vendor that smelled and tasted great but probably wouldn't pass Maw-Maw's cleanliness test.

As we got up to our hotel room, out our window we noticed a long line of people on the street waiting to get in to an establishment. We wondered what could be so good that people would wait that long?

The next day we went back to the ballpark. We had bleacher seats for the second game. Sitting in the Wrigley bleachers was quite the experience. It was like a block party. There were people out there who didn't know what sport was being played, much less the score. But they were having a ball.

We were there early for batting practice. We were sitting with a hot dog and a drink and kind of halfway watching the batters hit some bombs. Then, all of a sudden, everyone around us starts to stand. My dad stands up, reaches over and "smack".

A batting practice home run ball off the bat of Robin Ventura whistled into his outstretched hand. It caromed off his hand like it was made of stone. The ball rolled away and was never seen again. He called an error, although in fairness catching a ball hit that hard with one bare hand would be a highlight grab. I asked how his hand was and he dismissed me and said it was fine.

About fifteen minutes later, I asked the same question again.

"Oh, it hurrrrts," he said with a whimper.

We did have a good time out there. We watched the bleacher creatures heckle Mets' left fielder Rickey Henderson who would miss pitches while he was turned around yelling at the fans. After the game we went down near the field and took some photos. It was such a memorable trip.

We went back to the hotel and cleaned up a bit. We decided we wanted a taste of Chicago and decided on pizza. We headed down to the concierge, told them what we were doing and what we were after. He told us about this great place nearby. I joked to my dad that it was probably the place with the line around the block. The concierge said, "oh, so you saw it?"

We weren't interested in waiting all night for a pizza and asked if there were alternatives?

He said, "wait right here". He came back a few minutes later and handed us his business card with a hand-written message on the back. He said to hand it to the doorman.

At this point, we had to see what would happen. We strolled right past about a block and a half of waiting patrons. We strolled up to the doorman and handed him the card. He read it and said, "stand right here".

About three minutes later, he reappeared. Come with me. And you could feel the eye daggers from the line as we walked right in to our table.

That message, what did it say?

"VIPs, please take care."

So today is Father's Day. It is a day to stir up memories. Some good, some maybe not as much. But this is a year where I am thankful for the opportunity. Lots of people out there can't talk to their dad, their mom, their sibling, their child, their spouse. I spent the weekend with my dad.

We went out to dinner. We swam. And you guessed it, we watched some baseball. And I'm left with this message for all you visiting with loved ones today ...

VIPs, please take care.

She sits alone at the kitchen table, alternating between giggling and crying. Her dad comes back into the room to check to see which emotion is causing the latest outburst. She's been through a hellish year. No verbal outlet. No translator. No one to anticipate her needs.

She has to feel isolated, frustrated, abandoned.

But we don't really know how she feels. It is all conjecture.

She lost her mother ten months ago. The young woman, Madison, is nineteen. Her test scores suggest she is a decade younger. Her ability to overcome obstacles suggest she is much older. Her father finds her laughing and joins her at the table. He prefers Madison's infectious laugh to the hurt in her crying eyes.

They sit and "talk".

"Did you like the boiled eggs added to the salad," he asks? "Yes or No?"

"Yes."

"Did you like the cheesecake? Yes or No?" He already knew this answer.

"Yes!"

"Are you happy or sad?"

"Happy girl."

Even when she is sad, she often answers that she is happy. She tends to associate happy with good and sad with bad. This isn't an autism trait. Sometimes, her dad does this too.

It is exhausting being sad. Sometimes being sad seems like a job. One that we take breaks from but come back to. Eventually, we have those magic days where we don't clock in. But overall, we put in enough time at "work" to stay on the payroll.

Madison is still sad a lot, despite how she answers her dad. She looks over at a photo of her mom.

"I know you miss Mommy. It is OK to be sad. It is OK to be happy. Dad is sad sometimes and happy sometimes. That is how it will be for a while."

She stares intently. She is listening. She understands a lot but just how much, no one really knows.

"Do you understand?"

"Understand."

It is quiet in the house. They move into the living room. A baseball game is on.

"Do you want to watch baseball? Watch or change?"

She kind of smirks. She knows her Dad likes baseball. She wants him to be happy.

"Watch baseball."

But she doesn't watch baseball. She pulls out her phone and headphones.

Then she gets up and moves next to her dad on the couch.

She looks up at him and smiles.

"Happy or Sad," she asks?

Happy man.

They say you can get used to anything. They say in time you will get there. The man supposes he hasn't reached that destination yet.

It is early Saturday morning. The house is so damn quiet. The only sound is Madison's rocking chair, 'creek, creek'. Some noises are not to be fixed. The man remembers when he liked silence. It's like the time he ate so many blackberries he couldn't stand them anymore. He's had his fill.

He talks. His voice bounces off the walls. Madison doesn't answer. Because, well, she doesn't answer. So, he moves into the kitchen. He talks to Alexa. She plays some music. He bangs around in the kitchen. He starts to cook eggs and bacon. And coffee. There's noise now. He misses noise.

These lazy weekend mornings with nowhere to be, those arrive in a cloak of loneliness.

Suddenly, Madison shrieks. Is that a laugh or a cry? Here we go … and he shifts from chef into parent. It turns out she is giggling. He comes back into the kitchen. "Didn't I have coffee somewhere? I think I can still taste it? I did make it, right? Where is it?"

He checks the bacon. He drops the oven mitt into the oven. Madison runs into the kitchen and stops just behind him as he hangs over the oven fishing the oven mitt out. That heavy feeling in his chest returns. He's suddenly overwhelmed.

That's a feeling he is used to. It's sort of like a hug from an enemy.

His eyes fill. He has no idea why. But really, he does.

He's alone.

Ten months apparently isn't enough; not for quiet houses; not for early mornings; and not for waking up in bed alone.

He takes a deep breath. Madison sees his sad eyes. He sees her recognition. He cringes. He didn't want this. She runs out of the kitchen and flies into her rocker. This is hard for everyone.

An upbeat song starts. Music seems to affect him now more than before. He forces himself to sing along.

If this were "The Voice", none of the judges would turn around; not even Blake.

But he flips the switch. He dries his eyes, blows his nose. He's in parent mode again.

He checks on Madi. She's got her headphones on, perhaps saving herself from her dad's voice. She does see his energy, his "normalcy" and frees an ear. She smiles. He needed that smile.

They move back into the kitchen. They fix their breakfast. They eat every bite, hungry for a side dish of sustenance with their heaping plate of solitude.

He finds his coffee.

The heavy chest feeling has moved on to hug someone else.

We walk past the wallets, the t-shirts and the alligator heads. Past the Cajun spices, hurricane mix and key chains. Then we get smacked ... right in the memory.

Madison and her dad went to New Orleans Sunday. Her mom loved New Orleans, so her dad had been delaying this trip.

"Acme Oyster House, New Orleans, oysters, catfish, French fries, ketchup, sierra mist."

For someone who "doesn't talk", that's pretty descriptive. Madison has been making this request for months. Her dad would respond with, "it's too far. Maybe later".

A few weeks ago, Madi made her Acme request and before her dad could answer, she added this suffix, "too far, maybe later".

Ouch.

So here we are in the French Market. We made the trip with friends. Madi's dad felt having just the two of us would be an extended one-way trip to Memoryland, a place we need to get into, get out of, maybe dip in again and exit back. Having others there seemed to help.

The trip is hard for Madison. She has a lot of anxiety as we start the journey. At this point, there are just the two of us in the car. I try to take a selfie of us and it takes six photos to get one where she isn't making a frowny face. You can't grieve pretty.

So, we stop.

"Madison, are you sure you want to go to New Orleans? You seem really upset. Do you want to go to New Orleans or go back home?"

"New Orleans", she answered without hesitation.

"I know there will be a lot of memories of Mommy," her dad says. "She loved to go to New Orleans. But Mommy would want you to be happy and enjoy some of the things she liked. And find some new things you like. Do you understand?"

"Understand. New Orleans. Drive." And she points to the highway. It is given as a command. Dad was wasting time. Besides, doesn't he know it's far away?

If this were a sitcom, the "dad-talk" would have totally saved the day. She would have perked right up, and we'd have been singing about rainbows and lollipops all the way there and back. In real life, we had no such luck.

The memories are thick, especially walking through the French Quarter. Every shop that Hannah always wanted to slip into; every "haunted" this or "ghost" that, it is now wasted. The pralines from the candy shop Hannah liked, one of our friends hates. The dresses she always thought were so pretty, we just walk straight by. There were many things, more out of habit, that would have been pointed out that now feel awkward. Some are mentioned, some are swallowed. Some sit heavy on the chest.

Madison isn't the only one affected. Her dad keeps banging his head on low hanging memories as well. We are now at the point where every little thing isn't a painful reminder. Some memories are funny or make us smile. People said this would happen and they were right. Every memory is no longer painful.

One assumes each subsequent trip to New Orleans (or anyplace special to our past) will get a little easier as new memories supplement the old ones. But all this is new.

We eat at Acme, which was Hannah's favorite restaurant, and where Madison wanted to go. We wait eleventy-thousand hours for beignets at Cafe Du Monde. We stroll Bourbon Street. We watch street performers. We shop at the French Market where we make one purchase.

Many years ago, we found this Cajun seasoning that we liked called "Joe's Stuff". Hannah used it on nearly everything. She also made this dip that was mostly sour cream mixed with the seasoning. Madi really liked the dip. On Hannah's final trip to New Orleans, she bought the industrial size drum (only slight exaggeration) of this favored seasoning.

Sometime that next night, Madi awakened and decided she wanted dip. She pulled out a big bowl, emptied a large container of sour cream and overflowed the entire contents of Joe's Stuff into her "dip". Most of it went on the counter and the floor. When we awakened to see the aftermath, all we could do was grin and bear it. Hannah rolled with those moments.

And she did so without Joe's Stuff.

Madi's dad tells this story as he makes the purchase. Everyone laughed as he told it.

When they get home, Madison's dad asks her about the trip.

"Was New Orleans fun?" Yes, she answers.

"Was New Orleans also sad?" She waits. Then says, "Mommy, gone, sad".

"I know baby. It was a hard day. You are strong though. Mommy would be very proud."

"Strong." She repeats. "Proud."

Her dad is proud too. So proud that he is in the kitchen.

Anyone care for some dip?

He is cooking. And not just hamburger helper and frozen pizzas. This is the same guy who needed a recipe to boil water.

This both makes him proud and confused. Tonight, he experimented with oysters and made a pasta concoction that wasn't hideous. As the dish took shape, he couldn't help but think of someone who would have been surprised, but yes, she would also have been impressed.

He is at the point where random things pop up that remind him of his late wife. The other day he got in the car and the gas light was on. This hasn't happened in ten months. It used to happen all the time because someone would take whatever vehicle had the most gas in the tank and leave the other for her husband. Then bring home that car on empty and use the other – since her husband had just filled it with gas.

He can't walk through his home office without being stopped in his tracks. He stuck the photos from the funeral service in there months ago and they have claimed a spot. It's a collage. So many memories. If he sees it, it is like a magnet and he can't break away.

There are television shows, movies and songs that transport him back as well. He expects those. But making up an oyster recipe on the fly, while his daughter waits not-so-patiently, that is a bit unexpected. This isn't a memory. This is a missed opportunity for a memory. He isn't sure which he prefers.

Madison is happy when the dish is finally in front of her. She gobbles the food down, then looks over at her dad and says, "heartbroken". The words are heavy. Apparently, you could feel it in the air.

They are sharing more than a meal tonight.

Grief moves in like a storm. Sometimes after the squall passes, if you look hard enough you can find a rainbow. Today, he notices symbolic rainbows that were overlooked before. They are there if you look for them, just as sadness and gloom are readily available. He can't help but think braving this storm will somehow pay off someday.

Today's life is so different. He now does things

routinely he rarely, if ever did before. Like shop and unload groceries. Like shave his daughter's legs (that's freaking work, y'all) and book her doctor's appointments. Like lay in bed alone and imagine hearing footsteps on the stairs. And make up a recipe and find it makes his daughter sad.

They travel together through this journey, past the dashboard gas lights, the photo collages, the improvised meals alone. While the bumps in the road slow them down, a quick peek over their shoulders remind of the distance they've covered.

If you don't check the mileage, sometimes you forget where you started. Plus, you never know what strange location you travel into.

Like the kitchen.

"Madi, can you put the milk up?"

They are unloading groceries, father and daughter. The daughter is an impulsive shopper. The father vainly tries to reign her in. He isn't particularly successful, and the result is an aircraft carrier load of vittles.

The dad, like every man who has ever lived, tries to carry all of the groceries from the car to the kitchen in a single trip. Part man, part pack mule, you can't see his arms underneath bundles of plastic bags. His daughter helps, like members of the fairer sex often do, by carrying a single bag with a single item. Her bag contains a carton of milk.

The man drops everything onto the counter in a heap. She stands there and waits to hand him the milk, as if to check it in and get a receipt. He tersely issues the command, "Madi, can you put the milk up?"

He doesn't supervise the activity. She knows where the milk goes. While he is going through the bags and putting a few things in the pantry, he hears the fridge door open. It stays open a few seconds, presumably to find the perfect parking lot for the milk. When he turns around, the fridge is closed, and she is scurrying out of the room to cure cancer or feed the homeless or listen to Taylor Swift, all way more important than helping put away "more" of the groceries.

Dad finishes putting everything else in its place and they enjoy the evening.

The next morning, Madi wants breakfast. Her dad scrambles into the kitchen and starts to prepare what would have likely resulted in a blue-ribbon award-winning bowl of cereal. He pours the Fruit Loops into the bowl – when did they add marsh mellows to them? So much for the classics. He opens the fridge door and scans for the milk.

But he can't find the milk. He remembers shopping for it. He grabbed the one with the mid-July expiration date. Where could it be? It's not on the top shelf. He looks past a glorious package of bacon, over the ranch dip – now with cilantro - and moves aside the container of grape-pineapple-turnip-cactus juice concoction someone just had to have. The milk isn't in there. He even checks the freezer side. Nada.

Then he remembers, Madi put the milk up.

"Madi, where did you put the milk?"

She walks purposely over to the open refrigerator, closes the door and grabs the milk off the roof of the fridge.

She put the milk UP.

She was so proud. Dad, however, was a smidge frustrated as he grabbed the July room temperature container.

"Madi, I know Dad told you to put the milk up, but it has to go INSIDE the refrigerator to keep it cold. If not, it spoils and is yuck. We now have to throw it away."

Mean ol' Dad drops the milk, unopened, into a

garbage can.

Madi looks at him like he has three heads.

So, he retrieves the milk from the trash, opens the top and pours a few globs into a cup.

We can't drink that. She sees it and says, "Yuck". She puts the top back on and drops it back into the garbage.

We all feel like Madi with the milk at times. We try to follow what we believe we are supposed to do only to be rewarded with a cup of yuck.

Sometimes, we need someone to show us the way. Often, telling us gets us only so far. After all, she did as she was told. She put the milk up. It wasn't what her dad meant. He wasn't clear. Sometimes we say things that are obvious to us but others, through their different perspectives, just don't quite comprehend.

Our girl is gaining independence. She is always listening, trying to process. She understands her dad is trying to be mom too along with his regular dad duties and needs her help. She will get more opportunities. She will learn about dairy and refrigeration and expiration dates. She will understand that her dad, like most people she will converse with, doesn't always communicate intent.

So, they stand there looking in the open fridge deciding on plan B for breakfast. They work together to prepare bacon and eggs.

As they start to wrap up, her dad asks without thinking, "Madi, can you put the eggs up?"

He starts laughing immediately, thinking back on the night before.

"Madi, can you put the eggs back into the fridge?"

See, Madi isn't the only one learning.

She's beside her dad wearing her mom's pearls, lying in her mom's bed. It has been quite a morning.

Grief ebbs and flows like the tides. This morning – well, the entire weekend really – brought surfer quality waves.

Madison is upset. She isn't hungry. Her dad made her waffles. She isn't tired. She just woke up. She is agitated, hurling nonsense chants that may mean something to her but are lost in translation. These are the mornings where her dad really needs help. This goes on for many minutes, screaming, crying, frustration.

He is mostly patient. But we all know patience isn't awarded in endless supplies. He hits his limit with these words, "Hannah Puzak Etheridge, pretty."

A few months ago, Madison did this thing where she picked a different woman to identify with for a day. She was Katy Perry and Taylor Swift and Lindsay Lohan. She was also girls from her class. This finally fizzled out a few weeks ago. It came back today, with her mother's name.

Hearing those words came as a gut punch for her dad, sending that acid flowing through the belly that used to have permanent residence but now is back to a sporadic stay in the guest room. It kicked in the door today.

He had plans for this day. He was going to deep clean a bathroom and paint it. That will wait. Neither of them is up for that now.

She continues to cry. Her dad goes into a closet and pulls out a box. It has her mother's jewelry. She goes through it. She focuses on a pearl necklace and slips it on. She adds a ring, a bracelet and some clip-on ear rings. All go great with pajamas, by the way.

A friend is coming over later. Madison is asked what she wants to do today?

"Shop," she says.

Where do you want to go?

"Kohl's," she answers, surprising her dad.

What do you want to shop for?

"Black shirt," she says between sobs.

She used to go with her mom to Kohl's. Dad has never been in there.

A black shirt, huh? I bet it will look really nice with her mother's pearls.

Madison Etheridge, pretty.

Sometimes you just click.

Through life people float into and out of your life. New people emerge. You lose touch with others. There are some people who manage to stick around, either through proximity or a special connection.

Some people you might not like initially, wish they would just go away, but they find a way to win you over and eventually you can't imagine your life without them. With others, the friendship is like a cool drink on a hot day. It just feels right.

Having a loyal friend is difficult. It can be work at times. Friends don't always agree. Some bicker and exchange insults so often you wonder if they even like each other.

But having that friend you know is there proves invaluable. Most of us don't rely on them all that often, but the knowledge they are there when and if you do is invaluable. A close friend can be like that spare tire in the trunk. You may go a while and not need it, but when you need it … you really need it.

When Hannah passed, I learned a lot about the people around me. Death isn't a comfortable topic for most of us. Fortunately, most people don't have vast experience dealing with the loss of those close to them. When we do, it makes us feel awkward, clumsy – when all we want to do is show grace.

I remember Hannah's memorial service like it was yesterday. Standing in the front of that funeral home, that might hold 100 people, as five or six times that many poured through. People from every stage of our lives came. Childhood friends, college friends, former and current co-workers, people I met through writing and many people who knew Hannah's, or my families came to pay their respects.

To a person, they came up to the receiving line with sadness and caring in their eyes. They said some words, very few of which I can recall. But what I remember is the turnout, many of the faces, and at a time where I felt most alone that there were so many people there who wanted nothing more than to hug that pain away. Recalling that scene brings back a lump in my throat and heaviness in my chest. Grief can be as much physical as mental. But I'm proud so many people cared enough to show support.

Good friends are hard to find and even harder to maintain. Losing them hurts. It creates a hole where it was whole before.

My mother and my father each lost a good friend this week. There is one fewer person in each of their lives creating smiles, giving hugs and helping stave off that alone feeling during low points.

"I am ready for some good news," my dad told me on a phone call a few hours after losing his friend.

I couldn't render any.

Right now, words don't seem to help much; at least not any I can give. Regardless of our various life experiences, we struggle to comfort grieving spouses, children and others close to the deceased.

Yes, through life people float into and out of your life. Those we connect with become a part of us, a part we can hold onto forever and pull out front and center whenever we need it.

Sometimes we just click. The friendship was easy.
Now comes the hard part … saying a final goodbye.

He sits alone in the kitchen. His companion Alexa
plays Luke Combs. Madison is in the living room, fed,
not fussing. She let him sleep past seven, then burst
into his room with a face full of makeup, "Good
Morning!".

It is a Saturday morning. He is monitoring a work
software cutover. He sips coffee from a red cup that
says, "Get Your New York On", one of the world's
noisiest places. But his house is so quiet, especially
compared to this time a year ago.

The mornings can be tough. Coffee can be warm and
delicious but not a great conversationalist. As he
ventures out, he finds himself listening more, talking
less. Making small talk seems more difficult.

With only Madison to converse with, he understands
why.

His daughter misses the conversations too. For years
she sat there listening to her mother and father chat
away. Talking about work or sports or jokes or bills or
life. Now, her dad keeps most of that to himself and
Madison misses the noise, the banter. Seems they
can't hear anything over the quiet.

Her father tells her about the plans for the day. Her grandmother is coming. They will get out and do something later. She likes getting out. But more than that, she likes the conversations. When they visit with friends and family, she seems her happiest.

He has noticed that when he picks her up from camp and they are heading home, she is agitated. When they are going somewhere other than home, she is content. She doesn't want to go home. To solitude. To a house packed with memories.

For someone with a communication disorder, our girl really craves social interaction. Even if she is often only a spectator. Her dad understands. He misses the household bustle. He misses mindless small talk. He doesn't remember life before his late wife entered it and even nearly a year later, he is adjusting.

It's not just companionship he lacks. Now it begins to turn to the trivial things that he associates with her. Getting fussed at for loading the dishwasher "wrong". Picking up breakfast on the way back from a morning run. He hasn't eaten boiled crawfish since before, because she had remarked to him before she died that it had been too long since she had some. It's so strange how the brain works.

Madison pops into the kitchen and flashes a smile. His eyes water and he doesn't know why. She is in the best mood, excited about the day.

So, they talk.

They review the plans for the day. He discusses options. He plans to grill lunch. Perhaps, they will go out to dinner. Madison listens. She echoes back what she hears. There is chatter. The house isn't as quiet.

He refreshes his coffee. He loads the dishwasher, probably the wrong way. She looks on, smiling again.

She's right. It is a good morning. He just needed reminding.

A co-worker lost his wife over the weekend. She was mid-thirties. She left his world suddenly, within a span of a few days progressed from diagnosis to hospice to obituary. She leaves behind a grieving husband, two small children and a deep hole to fill.

Hearing this kind of news is painful for everyone. People expect me to reach out. I feel compelled to comply.

"If anyone can relate to what he is going through, it is you," a common friend says.

The friend isn't wrong. This is now an area of "expertise"; a skill no one asks for, a membership in a club with a steep entry fee.

We men don't like to talk about our grief. Talking about our feelings is sometimes considered confusing or less-than-masculine. We like to "do stuff", not "talk about stuff". But you know, we feel and hurt like anyone else. And this kind of loss brings a special kind of pain.

You hurt for your family and for yourself, for the loss of your partner, and all she would ever be.

You were a husband and now, you aren't, a shock to your identity. You feel less than whole, like a part of you that you were not even aware existed has disappeared, like an old pirate scratching an itch on a wooden leg.

Sure, you knew you cared. You knew you would be sad. You knew you would grieve. But the physical pain this kind of loss can cause was a surprise for me.

Someone is sitting on your chest. You wish they would get up, or diet ... or just go ahead and squash you. There's an acidic wave riding through your gut. It comes and goes. I assume it always will. Mine reappeared when I heard this news, ripping apart a wound that hasn't yet closed. You are not happy to reacquaint with this feeling, because it drops the baggage off at the front door and expects you to lug it around with you during its stay.

The body provides these unwanted reactions, but it can also rise to the occasion. I slept less than eight hours total in the first six nights. I seldom ate. I knew both were needed but food had no taste and the mind was too frenzied to rest. I closed my eyes and instead of snores, out came wails. Despite all that, I made good decisions. I planned a service. I dealt with visiting friends and family. I even parented in an impossible situation. The point is that while grief undoubtedly punishes your being, the body can also rise to the occasion and allow you to adrenaline push through the darkness.

Until you crash.

I remember the first night I slept. A friend and I visited another buddy's beach house. My mother stayed with Madi and I got out of the house, Hannah's house. This was around a week after the world changed.

Looking back, it was a great decision to get out of the house, during the worst week of my life. They forced me to laugh. I tried not to cry. It didn't matter that I failed. They just listened. I knew I wasn't alone.

We ate. I had two beers and sat down on the couch. I woke up six hours later in the exact same spot. They just left me there, like a department store mannequin. I felt a little better the next day – a first recovery step in this marathon of grief.

I wish I knew how to help this family. I'm good at words but words didn't really help me. We men, we often struggle with that kind of stuff. I received help with meals. With childcare. With household chores. With errands. With job flexibility. These fall into the "do stuff" category and I saw the value there. I see it now.

Grieving is different for everyone. Some of us want to be left alone. Others want our inner circle there. Some want to establish a new normal as quickly as possible. I needed that routine to help the transition into being a single parent. It is natural to feel alone right now. It is natural to feel overwhelmed and assume it is all up to you to figure out the new reality. People want to help. People need to help. Let them.

For me, with the risk of sounding like a certain football coach, it was a process. It is still a process.

I don't have a magic spell to make the chest feel lighter or cleanse away the grief. Just know that it does get easier not because you care any less but because you learn how to persevere, how to exist in a life you didn't choose without a person you wanted to share your life with.

Almost a year ago, I sat where you are now. Still a bit

lost, still a tad lonely but hope has returned.

Hope. It's how you fill that hole.

Someone referenced the term, out of body experience. Usually, I shrug at phrases like that.

Today, it seems to fit.

The man stands with his family in the funeral home, with hundreds of onlookers patiently lined to pay their respects. So many whispers. So many sad expressions.

"He looks like he's in a daze," one lady said.

"That's a thousand-yard stare," a co-worker describes.

One by one, people file by and pay their respects to the man whose wife has died. Most of the comments are not eloquent. Most people don't know what to say. They all feel empathy. They all want to do something, anything to help. Most ask if there is anything they can do. Words, especially now, are just window dressing.

Today, the man at the receiving end of the long line of grievers wasn't me. But at the first glimpse of him, I was him. He was me. That out of body experience thing, it sure felt real.

Reflecting on Hannah's service, that day it felt like there was someone else greeting all those people. Her death wasn't real at that point, and there was (and is) processing to be done. That day it seemed I was perched above watching, or even standing in that very line to greet the widower – this man I barely recognized - or maybe just somewhere else entirely. The mind helps you handle trauma in various ways and that was the chosen coping mechanism at that moment.

Today, I switched places again. I felt like I was the man receiving guests. My mind starts racing to devise a plan for what I will say to all these people. I was transported back in time eleven months and north 150 miles.

Then reality returns and someone else is in that lead role. I am relieved.

And now, instead of others making awkward comments, it is my turn.

I want to state how I imagine he is in a fog at the moment, how he is overwhelmed. And while I want to avoid intruding, I am in a position to offer suggestions of things that helped or things to avoid from my own experience. And how I can provide a non-judgmental listener. And that I have nearly a year head start on this journey he is about to take, even though the two situations have their differences.

Instead, my words are clumsy. I grapple to recall the word, "intrude", the word eludes me completely until minutes later. My eyes water, my throat gets raspy and I muddle through the message. Walking away, I'm bothered by my lack of composure.

And then it hits ... when you are in his spot, you don't remember what most people say. You remember who came, and how they spoke from the heart, often clumsily. I'm sure some visitors provide perfectly delivered pitches but none of that registered for me. And this is comforting, knowing all he will likely remember from my bumbled dialogue was that I attended the service and offered support from a position of common experience.

Perspective can be as valuable as it is elusive.

There is ample time to craft a message, a do-over. Grief isn't in the quick-fix business.

At the end of the service, the casket is wheeled down the aisle. He walks behind, head up, expressionless. I recognize that stare, or rather that feeling while giving this look. I feel like a voyeur, peering in on a man at rock bottom, traveling to a place I recognize but never want to return.

I turn away.

Then I stop, teetering on the brink of feeling sorry for myself. Ashamed of my selfishness, I turn back towards the scene. The man following that casket, it isn't me. And while I can transport back there – perhaps a little easier than I'd like – my journey is much farther along than his. This glimpse is a stark reminder of where I was, where I am now, but also displays I am nowhere near the place I want to be.

A friend checks on me.

"I'm OK," I mutter. "I can't help but take myself back there during this scene."

"I imagine so," the friend replies. "I hope he understood and remembers some of what you said to him back there. Your experience can really help him."

Then adds, "Unlike you, most of us don't know what to say in these moments."

Clumsy as it was.

Author's Note: Below is a powerful story about the struggle facing the parents of a childhood friend.

She says she hates his beard and so would he. It does seem to make him happy now though.

Alzheimer's has robbed her of her father. But there are glimmers of his personality that shine through. Then a few minutes pass and he's gone.

This is him, day after day.

He is going to the mountains this weekend. He likes to look at the leaves turning colors. However, they won't even be home yet, and he'll tell his wife they should go to the mountains. There's no credit for yesterday, for even an hour before. It is all about now.

His wife, she bears the brunt of the caretaking. He's a big man, a former college athlete. Helping him with basic needs is no picnic. He is dependent on her. She does the best she can. What choice does she have? To her, in sickness and in health is not just lip service.

They have discussions. He offers sound judgment. That guy in this body, he once ran a mill. There's a smart man in there somewhere. But he's not the same person, not with any consistency anyway.

He knows he gets confused, but he isn't really aware of the gravity of his condition. This started nine years ago after a blow to the head at work and has progressed steadily.

He asks questions. Did you pay this bill? Did you go the store? When are the kids visiting? She answers the same questions over and over again. He gets animated about her making decisions without consulting him. She explains they just spoke about it minutes earlier. And the day before. And the week before that. He doesn't remember. He's confused. She's patient but heartbroken.

On the wall are photos of their children and grandchildren. He asks about the grandchildren's names? Who did their son marry? Did their daughter have her baby yet? He asks. She answers.

Then he asks again.

Yet, he can remember high school classmates, college football games he participated in, stories from the 70's. His short term is the shortest of terms.

His story is becoming more and more common. He suffered multiple concussions during his college football days. You hear all the stories about CTE and how it impacts many of his peers. His daughter can't help but wonder if he took one lick too many.

His wife, his sons, his daughter, they all wish they knew more to help him. They wish they had some answers. They wish he could remember.

It's like that movie, "Fifty First Dates," his daughter explains. Every day is starting over. Except there's no laugh track, no happy ending. And at the end of the movie the rest of us return to our lives while they have another first date.

There is a love story though.

His wife is there every day. It's a job she can't call in sick to. Each week gets harder instead of easier. She does it out of love, out of loyalty, out of necessity. Even when her own sickness, and folks she is fighting cancer, has a day where it gets the best of her. Yet she pushes. She has to. He is depending on her.

Her devotion inspires. She's earned a break. A son books a cruise, her first. If anyone deserves a break, a cancer-fighting, Alzheimer's caretaker has to be pretty damn high on the list.

This disease has taken away a husband, a father, a grandfather and a personality.

He is excited, playing with his baby grandson. Around ten minutes later he will ask if this grandson has been born.

The beard, though, is still there. It seems to be one of the only mainstays.

"He was always clean shaven," his daughter explains.

"He always smelled like Old Spice. Now he doesn't want to shave. His entire personality has changed."

This weekend they head to the mountains. He wants to see the leaves.

He wants to see the leaves.

He wants to see the leaves.

He went to see her Sunday. She didn't have much to say so he carried the conversation.

He discussed their trip up. They had a shrimp boil and grilled oysters with her family. The food turned out great and everyone had a good time. They told stories, some of them about her, and although there were some close calls, everyone held back their tears.

He tells her about some projects around the house. How he has made plans and tells her stories only she would appreciate.

He talks about their daughter. How she is maturing. How she misses her mom. How she keeps her dad guessing. How they both really could use her help.

"I know you are watching over Madison," he says. "I imagine you may be looking over me as well. If so, if it isn't too much trouble, I'd love some guidance."

He tells her about this new chapter in his life, one he feels a little sheepish discussing with her. But then again, he is talking out loud in a cemetery. He realizes this may seem odd if anyone was watching.

Over the last quarter century, he discussed with her everything from important things like job relocations to something as quirky as which shirt goes with hammer pants. This is a new topic for him to divulge. He tells her about a new friend.

He asks for guidance. He doesn't know if he will get it, or if he does, will he even recognize it.

He says his goodbyes and hops in his truck. A song is just beginning, "My Best Friend", by Tim McGraw. He smiles to himself and thinks, she really was his best friend. And in the end, they were certainly more like friends than anything hot and steamy. Twenty-something years together can do that. But they rarely had a day where they weren't constantly conversing, like best friends.

He heads to campus and goes for a run. He thinks about his earlier chat, remembers a half dozen more things he forgot to tell her, before he eventually clears his head. He gets back in the truck to a radio filled with static. He barely notices. He starts to drive.

As he nears the cemetery, the static clears. A song starts up, at nearly the beginning. It is Lanco's "Born To Love You". This time, the song selection gives him pause. Out of all of the song choices that could have been played – no country girl shaking it or beer guzzling summer days – it was probably just coincidence that this song with these lyrics fight through the static?

"Born again in a church where the steeple's white
Preacher preach Book of John and my momma cried
Meaning of life was in verse two
Didn't make sense 'til I found you"

The song doesn't state what chapter, just what verse. Not exactly a biblical scholar, he Googles Book of John verse two and finds chapter 2, verse 2 is the famous Jesus turns water to wine story. Then he asks a friend, without context for an overview of that verse.

"Well, the changing of water to wine was the first miracle Jesus performed that made the disciples believe. It signifies that he could and would turn 'death into life'."

He gasps.

"It was a very powerful meaning and message," the friend continued. "Even though his disciples were unsure, Jesus said you will soon see for yourself. See back then the water was not safe to drink hence the wine was like purified for them. So, it has great symbolism turning what's dirty to something perfectly safe. Water, 'sin', into wine, 'forgiveness'."

He doesn't understand what has happened. He doesn't know if he is reading something out of nothing because he wants there to be meaning. He does know that he asked for guidance and he received a message.

Perhaps, that conversation wasn't as one-sided as he believed.

"Petunia.

"Petunia."

She keeps repeating this word. Her dad is clueless to what she means.

Madison often elicits nonsense words as kind of a repetitive coping mechanism. Or maybe it is her way of contributing to the conversation. But this seems different. She is using this word to communicate, but her dad is not responding.

He thinks about the flower, petunia. Maybe she saw it in a magazine, or online or television. Maybe there was a smell someone described as like a petunia. He thinks to himself, wasn't there a cartoon pig named Petunia? That's kind of random, though. Her dad realizes he isn't the most up-to-date on pop culture and acknowledges there could be a singer or actor or reality star with that name. Alexa, Google, no help. He can't figure it out and his daughter is getting frustrated.

These days as Madison talks more often, misunderstood exchanges are frequent. These moments are tough for her but also for the person trying desperately to break the code. Sometimes her dad feels as if he is solving a riddle, only there is no answer key if he can't solve it.

Only screams.

He wonders if petunia could be a food. They haven't eaten yet and they are in the kitchen.

"Use the clues you have, Dad," he thinks to himself. They walk together to the pantry. He mentions various foods and she just repeats them. Then asks what she wants to eat, and she says, "petunia".

"So, petunia is a food," he asks her rhetorically? "What do you eat with petunia?"

She hands him a loaf of bread. He says, "do you want a sandwich? Yes or no?"

"Yes," she says with excitement.

"A petunia sandwich?"

"Yes!"

"A tuna sandwich?"

"Petunia sandwich," she says. He laughs out loud to hear it.

They are both excited, relieved, connected. He hugs her.

He empties the tuna packet into a bowl, mixes in some mayonnaise and spreads it onto the bread.

She devours it.

Her dad smiles. A sense of accomplishment fills him, making his insides warm.

Their lives are filled with uncertainty, with disconnects, with frustration making a moment like tonight so much sweeter.

She communicated. He understood. They are progressing.

Petunia.

It's what's for dinner.

A long car ride. A dentist appointment awaits. Both passengers have anxiety about the day's activities.

Madison is getting a bit upset. Her dad reaches in the center console and pulls out lip gloss. He may be the only man in America with watermelon lip gloss stashed strategically throughout his world. She snatches the prize, unveils the makeup mirror from the sun visor and does her thing.

Her dad sneaks a peek over and swears he sees her mom's reflection look back smiling at him. He does a double take as Madison snaps the mirror cover closed. This hasn't happened before. He just shakes his head and smiles.

Like his daughter, he is going through many changes in his life. These unexplained moments are comforting, even if he thinks his brain is tricking him.

A few minutes later, the radio signal fades out. He scans the dial.

"Well you're a real tough cookie with a long history
Of breaking little hearts like the one in me"

He smiles again. Hannah used to sing that song to Madison. The chorus starts. Madison belts it out.

"Hit me with your best shot
Why don't you hit me with your best shot
Hit me with your best shot
Fire away"

And just like that, the signal fades away. They stick it out straining to hear the remainder of the song and then flip the dial again.

"Hey soul sister, ain't that Mr. Mister on the radio, stereo" and upon recognition Madison is performing that one too. Another reminder of her mom, a song they sang together.

And just like that, the trip improves. The seal is broken, and the pair relax.

Music plays such a big part in Madison's life. Her mom used that to connect with her, to calm her. The seed bore fruit once again on a day where she had to be strong.

Dental visits are tough on everyone. They are especially tough for people like Madison, who wouldn't let people touch her mouth or ears until she became a teenager. She has a mouth full of problems, and she is finally to the point they can be addressed.

This was always a sense of contention. Doctor visits

were difficult, and Hannah handled most of them alone. Dad worked and didn't carry his weight. He regrets that now. Sure, he was always there when asked, but in hindsight he picked his spots.

These days, he's unprepared and learning on the fly. He's overly emotional and doesn't understand why. He's usually pretty level, so the difference is noticeable and concerns him.

Madison, for whatever reason, handles the trip like a pro. She sits still for x-rays, re-positions her mouth on demand. She waits patiently while dad fills out forms and discusses options. Other than traffic delays that turn a long trip into a longer one, the entire day went just about as well as anyone could hope.

They are riding home. The anxiety is gone.

And now, there's no need to raid the console for lip gloss. There are also no musical connections, no quick glimpses of someone who isn't there. They can handle this part on their own. They feel confident now.

He starts quietly singing, "Hit me with your best shot. Fire away."

She is in the passenger seat, stiff, contorted, with her face doing unspeakable things. The doctors call it a grand mol seizure. Watching helplessly from the driver's seat is her father. He calls it hell.

Just a few moments earlier she had been singing along to a hair band song cut decades before she was born.

"Sweet Dreams are made of this", then she trailed off.

Now, she is mashed between the headrest and the car door, legs and arms both stiff. Her eyes are looking up into her brain, her jaw clinched.

This is hard to watch.

Her father tries to control her body with one hand, hoping to keep her safe in the seat. With the other hand, he steers the car to the shoulder of the road. The seizure seems to last 12 days, although the short hand has somehow only moved a few ticks.

Then as sudden as it started, the violence stops. Both of his hands are holding her upright in her seat. Her eyes normalize, but she isn't back yet. He talks to her.

"Baby, you had a seizure. How do you feel? Are you going to throw up? Here, drink some water. Put your head back and rest. Do you remember it?"

She doesn't respond, other than to swallow some

water.

"I'm sorry baby. Do you remember if we took your seizure meds last night?"

He starts to blame himself. Did they forget the night dose? They are in the middle of a home remodel and the routine is temporarily askew. The morning dose, he is sure she had. But a missing dose, is that why this happened? Is this horrible scene his fault?

He asks, "do you want to go see a doctor? Or go home?"

"Beach", she replies.

That was where they were heading.

"Babe, you had a seizure. I'm not sure the beach is a good idea."

"Beach," she says.

They sit for a few minutes. She starts to perk up. She pulls out her phone and starts playing a game. Then she sings along with the radio. If you walk up now, you wouldn't believe why they pulled over.

"Sorry," she says.

"Why are you sorry, Madi?"

"Seizure, sorry" … his heart sinks … "go to beach",
she adds.

So, they are at the beach. Dad is not proud of his
decision, but he is there just the same.

She stands in the water, maybe knee deep. Her dad
remains inside her shadow and follows her like a
puppy. She smiles. A wave pushes her down and she
laughs. They had not been the beach much this
summer. School starts soon, and the opportunities
are dwindling. She likes the beach, as did her mom.
Her dad likes it too, when he isn't playing medic alert.
This isn't your cliched, relaxing day at the beach.

He is troubled. He blames himself. He can't fix this.

If she is troubled, she hides it well. Dad coaxes her
out of the water and they head for some lunch. It
was her mom's favorite place. They enjoy a nice
meal. She smiles. No one would ever guess how
frantic things were earlier. It is an idyllic scene.

He can't believe his life.

A song plays.

"Sweet dreams are made of this
Who am I to disagree?"

He is thinking about his wife tonight. How she died. How she lived. How she didn't get to do many of the things she wanted to do. How her sudden departure robbed him of his planned future.

She died suddenly. There was no warning. No chance to ease into it. Just that scene in the Thomas Hospital waiting room with those words seared into his mind, "We were unable to resuscitate her". Months later, he remembers everything about how he found out.

She collapsed at work, where she was surrounded by people who cared about her. He is thankful for that, if you can call it that.

He is thankful she wasn't driving when she collapsed, wrecking her vehicle and perhaps taking someone with her, even their daughter. We might have never known what caused the accident. He is thankful she wasn't home alone with Madison, as would have been the case only an hour later. Our girl has enough to overcome without watching her mother die. While we will never know how Madison would have reacted to her mom's situation, her dad suspects he would have come home after the work day to a houseful of agony. He is thankful Hannah was at work, and not somewhere her presence couldn't be explained, or she wouldn't be found quickly. His mind drifts and flips into dark places, yet he is thankful.

Yes, thankful she collapsed at work, where help arrived and gave her a chance. She was brought back to life twice on the route to the hospital. Then despite their best efforts, could not be brought back in the emergency room.

He is thankful he wasn't tasked with saving her. While some of us husband/father types love to play the protector, the autopsy revealed there was nothing anyone could do. Seeing her panicked expression as she fought for her life is not an image he needed to experience first-hand. Imagining it is crushing.

He is even more thankful his daughter found out the way she did, in a hospital waiting room. She had to fear there was a problem, however nothing would prepare any of us for this shocking reality.

Six weeks prior, she was in the hospital room when her grandfather, Hannah's father, took his final breath. None of us understood how important that would be at the time. Hannah wanted Madison there to help her understand death. She knew Madison would eventually lose someone close to her and wanted her to experience it – reinforcing how visual she is. Madison was present for all of his funeral services as well.

This was a reference point, a baseline if you will, for both Madison and for her support group as they all processed Hannah's passing.

The family is moving through life day by day. It is difficult to look too far ahead. After a life without a sense of mortality, it is ever-present. How fortunate they were. How fortunate many of us are, dodging the big loss for many years. Eventually, it gets us all.

Again, he is thankful for the way this loss transpired. If it had to happen, protecting he and his daughter from the scene was fortunate.

Author's Note: This is another story about someone I met during the journey. She allowed me to share her story.

Her mother left when she was a toddler.

She grew up without the things mothers do for daughters like frilly dresses, fancy hairstyles and birthday cakes.

She wondered, "what is wrong with me that my own mother doesn't want me?"

Her childhood is hard. A child needs a mother. Her father isn't much for nurturing. She struggles into adolescence. She practically raises herself. She feels empty; like she doesn't matter. Left to fend for herself, she makes poor decisions. She faces addiction. Abuse – all kinds including the stuff that typically make people who hear of it angry enough to spit nails.

She is looking for something, anything, to make her feel alive. She marries. He is an addict. She has children. She wants to be the type of mother she never had. She works to change. She learns twelve steps. She is in recovery. She becomes the kind of mother that elicits pride. Her husband gets sober. Life is better. White picket fence, PTA, family vacations – it seems she is on her way.

Her husband stumbles, backtracks, then abandons her. She is left jobless, penniless, homeless, hopeless – with sets of little eyes watching her and needing a miracle.

Despite her despair, she does not relapse. She doesn't want to be that person, to let them down. After all, a child needs a mother.

She is now without her husband, who continues to make her life hell anyway he can. She tries to move on. Months turn into years and she scrapes by, largely on her own. It's hard. They don't have much but life continues. She excels at her job and gets promoted. Her kids respond to her love, her example and are great students and well-behaved.

But still, something is missing. She hasn't found companionship. She is about to give up on men when a new guy pops into her life.

This man, he asks her out to lunch. He makes her laugh. They go out again and again. He treats her like she is special, like she matters. She feels good about herself with him. They have chemistry. They talk for hours. She discusses her past. She is afraid he won't like what he hears and will run away. She is afraid she isn't good enough. Can she dare believe someone will love her for who she is, ignoring who she was? Will the recurring theme of abandonment reappear? Is her past destined to follow her, like a chain pulling her under water until finally she tires of swimming with it?

Similar to a broken plate reassembled with scars showing and glue visible, she knows choosing to love her isn't the easy path for him to choose.

But a funny thing happens. The man doesn't leave. They discuss who she is, who she was, and why. He likes the person she has become, regardless of how she got there. He tells her a story.

"There are times when I just want to eat the cake," he says. "It is beautiful, delicious and makes me happy. I love how this cake turned out. Yes, I realize that I don't like how the cake was made. That this is a recipe that chefs aren't going to want to emulate if they have a choice not to. But this cake is here, placed in front of me, and I really like this cake, regardless of how it got here."

She likes the story. She likes the message.

She finally gets her cake.

"MaaaaMaaaa. MaaaaMaaaa."

She's screaming these words at the top of her lungs.

Her dad can handle almost anything she does. She repetitively states foods, celebrities, people in her life. She says words that mean something different to her than to the rest of the world. She destroys furniture, leaves the milk out, and doesn't wait to talk during commercials when the game is ending. He rolls with it.

This morning is different. Her routine is disrupted. She spent last week at her grandmother's house. Her own house is in mid-remodel. New floors, wall paint, reconfigured furniture ... all with the goal of a quick sale and a fresh start across town. The upheaval is tough for both. This morning it caught up with her.

Her mother was her calm. Her peace. Her pillow in a rock garden.

Her father has his moments but he's not her mother. Some days a girl just needs her mama.

Her dad has been trying to talk to her. To explain again why the house is a collection of paint cans and furniture piles. He details her plans for the week. School starts Wednesday, which is an anxiety source, despite how much she enjoys going. She isn't eating her cereal. He can feel the wave approaching.

When she cries out for the person they both wish was here to comfort her, the words smack him, halt him and crumble him. He is swept away.

She goes without verbalizing her longing for her mother most of the time. He likes it that way, apparently, because he isn't proud of his response to her maternal request this morning.

He stops. Looks down and her cries fall down on him like punches, or maybe rain, or struggles in deep water. He can't fix this. He can't reason this away. He is overwhelmed, lost.

It is time for her to go to daycare. He tells her so, and she walks out to the car, still screaming.

A neighbor is walking by. The man sees Madison, then waves at her and her escort. Her dad composes, tries to stifle that feeling in his chest so he can return a wave and fake a smile. Time to face the public.

People often never know what goes on behind closed doors.

Our girl's public display continues as she wails on the way to her destination. At this point, her dad tries to bribe her with doughnuts. They stop and go in, to let her see the choices and pick what she wants. As they wait for service, Madison burst into tears again.

Everyone stares. A girl in the line lets us move ahead. Madison accepts her gesture and pushes up to the counter, blaring out a request for strawberry. She receives a strawberry doughnut with sprinkles and a diet coke. As Dad pays, a still crying Madison violently crams the doughnut into her mouth. The scene becomes someone's story, their morning water cooler conversation.

The pair match strides through the parking lot to the car. They sit for a minute. Dad guzzles from an oil drum-sized coffee cup that will be his commute companion for the hour-long trip to work. He thinks, there isn't enough caffeine to get him through this morning.

But as they drive to drop Madi off, the cries slow. She seems to right herself.

The wave is receding. They are both still standing, figuratively, as they sit side-by-side in the car.

As they pull into a parking spot, she says, "sorry."

Another impact.

And the tide sweeps him away again.

"Miranda Lambert, blonde hair."

She is screaming. It is early on a weekend. So early a rooster would grab the covers and roll over.

But she runs into his bedroom and does a full backyard slip-and-slide across the sheets.

The morning before, her father awoke with a random leg cramp about 5 AM and never went back to sleep. But this night, he was sleeping well, dreaming even. But that all changes quickly with her appearance. He is tired, frustrated, pissed. He grumbles like he is the Grinch who stole lazy mornings.

She's hungry, he guesses. He finds his feet are on the floor heading downstairs, with a shadow he can't shake. She's still chanting assorted celebrities and their respective follicle hues. The kitchen awaits.

There is a gruff bark at Alexa, "play country music."

She obliges.

"Sunday morning, man, she woke up fighting mad."

As the lyrics hit him, he laughs at their appropriateness.

His daughter doesn't see the humor. He decides to focus on what they can control. He feeds her breakfast. He gives her something for a tummy ache. She is still upset. Maybe it was the sudden waking or the musical inspiration, but he has an idea.

He walks into the room with an overflowing box of photos and puts them in front of her. He grabs a picture collage from her mother's service that has been hidden away. They are going to re-purpose it.

The collage has 20 photos of her mother. He thinks it would be better if there are pictures of others in there as well. So, he gives her a job.

"Madison, we need to pick out pictures of you that you like, and pictures of Mom, Dad, and others and we will put them in this frame."

Meanwhile, he takes the current photos out.

She has stopped fussing. She's curious what this breakfast making man has planned.

They get started. She does play-by-play for the process, stating the people in each picture with characteristics.

"Aunt Laurie, young. Ellie, baby.

"Mimi, brown hair.

"Nana, grandmother.

"TaTa, gone.

"Mom, sad."

She has a pile of 30 or so that she has selected. Dad helps decide which ones they will use based on how it fits directionally into the frame. He has a few he encourages her to add, including one where a toddler version of this young woman next to him is playing in the mud.

Then Madison excels. She tapes them into place. There may never have been a more thorough tape job. She goes through nearly two rolls of scotch tape. Dad just watches. She's enjoying this. He doesn't want it to end.

They put the finishing touches on it and stand it up. Remarkably, the tape holds.

There is another song playing, "That's what memories are made of."

He's so glad she got him up early this morning.

It is the hill that you can't seem to find the top.

The constant wind in your face that never seems to shift to your back.

We are a few days short of a year, that day that changed the lives of many. That news that forever altered a family, leaving a gaping hole we didn't know how we'd ever start to fill.

To say this year has been challenging for Madison and her dad is an understatement. Her dad can be prone to hyperbole. "This is the best shrimp boil ever." "This is the worst referee call I have ever seen." Most of the time, he's being dramatic.

This has been the worst time of my life. This is not debatable.

That said, there have been highlights mixed in between the gut punches. Some old friends reappeared and reconnected. Some new people appeared and are now close friends. Strangers swoop in to help your child – and there's just something that tingles inside you when that happens.

There were times when I played the "woe is me" card. I'd be lying if I didn't admit many nights spent in melancholy, in anger, in frustration – but the primary description to explain the past 12 months has been a feeling of being overwhelmed.

No one is ever prepared for what happened. No one handles this kind of loss, this kind of increased responsibility, this much loneliness without stumbling. This past week I fell.

Work has been an oasis for me. With my home life in chaos, house in full remodel, daily struggles with Madi, work was a respite, a break. The day was predictable, something I have experience with and can deal with the obstacles. Then the work conditions changed, and it became just another extension of chaos. I hit my limit Thursday when two groups had been arguing about a topic for a couple of days with no resolution. All that frustration came boiling over and they caught the wrath.

That same day, a sitter canceled. I had planned to go out with some friends and do a fantasy football draft. The "why" didn't matter, it was just a chance to get away and not be Dad, not be the boss, just be the person I used to be. This was the third sitter cancellation/no show in six days. It just felt like life was piling on. I snapped.

Madi had been struggling a bit in the mornings and evenings. That day I picked her up and just assumed the hard times would continue; Murphy's Law or Etheridge Luck or when it rains it pours. We got into the car, I exhaled heavily after picking her up as we prepared to drive home. I explained about the sitter not being able to make it. I explained Dad had a bad day at work, was missing his plans tonight and hoped we would find a way to have a good night any way.

A song she liked happened to come on the radio and she started to dance in her seat, which is not her normal behavior. She smiled and laughed. We got home. We ate. She went to her chair, got her phone and was content all evening. Not as much as a single whine or whimper. She went to bed and I thanked her.

Her dad desperately needed that break. I spent an hour pretty much undisturbed and did the draft online. I caught myself smiling later that evening. The roller coaster ride continues.

The next morning, I was talking to my mom and venting a bit about the week. I mentioned how Madi broke from routine and behaved near perfectly the night before.

"Do you think she can tell when you are upset? It seems like it has happened before," Mom says.

"It sure seems like it," I answer. "At this point she has surprised us all so many times, I'm not underestimating her anymore."

We continue to climb the hill, stumbles and all. Just as has been the case all year, you just never know where that helping hand will come from.

Her photo stares as he eats lunch. She's happy, smiling on a beach vacation. She did love the beach.

He has been busy this morning, disassembling things they built together. Life has torn them apart. The last tangible reminders of their lives together will vanish with a pending relocation. The souvenirs remain. The memories, the photos, the child they made together are all loud today. Still, she stares, quietly.

There have been many changes. If she popped back into this house today, she would need a map or guide to navigate. And not just the home, the two occupants as well.

So, what would he say if she were standing in front of him? Where would he start? How would he sum up these last dozen months without her?

He'd start by saying all is forgiven. For leaving so suddenly without transition. For lies, big and small, known and unknown. For always bringing the car back on empty and taking his, then bringing his back empty too. For the fights she picked, the ones she won - which were most of them - and for leaving dishes in the sink and clothes piled on the closet floor. For getting a cat even though he was allergic, then getting a second one.

Then he'd apologize. Apologize for not always listening to the intent behind the words. For not doing more to help her reach her dreams. For not being supportive of her ideas he didn't see the value in but were harmless. Of not doing more to bring them closer. Of often choosing his life over their lives. For never getting to realize the plans they made. For her not getting to wear that sweater that arrived a few weeks after she passed. And he'd come clean about that business trip where he had an incredible meal and downplayed it, so she wouldn't be jealous. For watching so many ballgames and so few chick flicks. And for being the one who remains to chase new dreams that she can't experience.

Then he'd tell her about their daughter. How hard it is for Madi without her mother. How she struggled badly, and still does today. But how far she has progressed, primarily because she had no choice. How she helps her dad with things no one would ever suspect. Like sparing his feelings, picking him up when he is down and understanding difficult situations. She understands death, and we didn't know if she would. How her school embraced her and how much she loves going there.

How she went first out of hundreds of seniors at graduation making her dad beam at how far she has come and cry at how you missed seeing it. And how she attended a couple of proms and wanted you there the entire time. We all did. How she waved and blew a kiss after seeing your body for the final time. Her mom took her a long way. She will lean on others to reach her destination.

And, yes, he would tell her about his year. How supportive his co-workers were. How strangers brought meals for months, and others sent gift cards and well wishes. How family stepped up, how friends went above and beyond to earn eternal gratitude. How he cried himself to sleep, when he slept. How he lost thirty pounds in a few weeks after she passed. How his entire self-image was destroyed. And he has rebuilt, stronger, more mature, wiser. And he will use this experience to be a better man, to help others in similar situations. To help those close to him. To help himself.

He is dating. She would want to know. He would describe the new lady as easy-going, patient, full of caring and positive energy. And quirky. Hannah loved quirky. He thinks they could have been friends.

It has been a year. The worst year. But he thinks she would be proud. That's all he ever wanted.

She smiles at him. He smiles back, with watery eyes.

Must be the cat allergies.

Hannah,

There were nights we wondered if we would make it this far. But like people kept telling us, it is amazing what you can accomplish when you aren't given a choice. Lots of support, some expected and others by complete surprise - and here we are one full year later.

This morning we sit alone in this house. Madi just had sushi for breakfast because, why not? Rest easy, your legacy is in good shape with her. She still loves the things she did with you, perhaps even more so now. She talks about you frequently. She tells people - but only those she trusts - that "mom is gone sad." I'm a words guy and I can't really say it any better.

This morning, I'm sipping coffee and thinking about how different our lives became with your tragic news. How overwhelmed we were, how much we depended on you, how all of our plans were shuttered.

Today we will head to see your family. It seems like the right move, and that intuition guides us. We will go by your resting place and chat some, just in case you can't check Facebook. We'll cook and laugh and tell stories. I know we will be sad, but we also want to celebrate your life.

So tomorrow we will do a concert, and I'll try to

scream half as loud as you would have. We'll make a memory for Madi, I promise you that.

I know you were probably afraid in those final moments. Afraid for your delicate condition. Afraid that Madi would be alone and lost. Afraid that I wouldn't be up to this task if something happened to you. You had cause to fear all of that and more.

Don't feel guilty. I had those same fears. But a year later, after plenty of stumbles, we are doing OK. We aren't flourishing, we aren't by any means a finished product, but we are together helping each other do life - with occasional assists from people who love us.

Yes, it has been a calendar year. In some ways it seems like only a few weeks, but then when we think about everything that has changed, you must have left us many, many years ago.

We sit here today a bit somber and reflective, but hopeful about our improbable progress. For August 30 is the day you died, and we have to acknowledge that.

One day you died, but the 44 years before that you lived. We need reminding at times, especially today. Love you,

Mark and Madi

It's 3:32 PM and he is graveside. He isn't sure why he felt this is where he should be, on the exact date and time she passed away. There is symmetry to it, to go back to her at the very instant a year later so she wouldn't be alone. So, he wouldn't be alone.

He thinks of that moment a lot, especially this week. There has been loads of time to reflect. He wishes he could have said goodbye. Odds are he would have blubbered through it, but he would have liked the opportunity.

This day started like so many others, with Madison bursting into his bedroom upset. He's grown accustomed to it, but he'd prefer the rooster crowing if given a choice. After a bit of a tussle, she calmed down. Then he loads up to head to Livingston and Bam, his car battery is dead.

He transfers everything to his truck; the battery will wait until he gets back. He gets gas and picks up a bag of ice for a cooler of food he is taking. About halfway across the parking lot, the bag bursts and ice scatters across Baldwin County.

He stands, looks up and says aloud to the universe at large, "Is that all you got? You picked the wrong guy on the wrong date. After last year on this date, a rough morning is nothing."

They get to Livingston and have lunch at the bakery where Hannah always took Madi. People asked how they are doing, and the significance of today is explained.

"Has it been a year already?"

It has.

As they head to the cemetery, Madison is asked if she still wants to go. She seems excited about it.

They pull up and walk to Hannah's headstone and sit Indian-style on the grass. It is a beautiful day with white, puffy clouds. It is hot. The ants are happy to have visitors.

Madi is asked what she would like to tell her mom? She sits silently. Her dad says he will start.

He explains how well Madison is doing in school. How her teacher says she is more interactive, with fewer meltdowns. How school is her calm zone, kind of like work is for her father. He discusses the home remodel, how everything looks different, and how they plan to relocate. He details their weekend plans, the concert, who they will see and when they return. He explains a few other assorted odds and ends and then turns to Madi, "do you have something you want to say to Mom?"

She sits quietly. You can almost see her thinking. Her dad is patient. She's working up to something and he really wants to hear it. He finally urges her again.

She finally blurts out ... "So sorry, Mom!" and begins to cry.

Her dad encourages her. His move may seem counter-intuitive, but this is a girl who is often stone-faced, and her emotional outbursts are accompanied with flailing arms and legs. This is different. This is deliberate. This is controlled. This is Madison dealing with her grief, or at least how she thinks she is supposed to.

They sit a while. He discusses how much her mom loved her. How many fun things they did; the things they shared. And how she needs to keep doing those things her mom liked. Do it for Mom.

Then he asked if she wants to go sit in the truck. She does. He cranks the engine and returns for a solo visit.

He checks his watch. It is almost the time, to the minute, when she departed. He discusses his regrets, his difficulty with the way things ended, his plans for the future. He explains he is trying to remember all of the good times while she was alive, and not focus on the one day where she died. And he struggles to do it. He asks for guidance. He asks for wisdom. He asks for support.

Then he turns and walks away. There is a song playing as he gets into the truck. It stops him cold.

It's Cole Swindell's, "Even Though We Break Up In the End" and it talks about how the artist would still pursue the relationship all over again, even though it ends badly.

The message washes over him, his eyes get splashy behind his shades.

And he says, "Thanks. Me too"

He is lazy today. Life is too much.

He has so much to carry. He pretends to be strong, sometimes he actually believes it. A teardrop sneaks out before he can catch it. He loses his patience. His stomach hurts. He stops pushing and takes a seat. The guilt piles as high as his responsibility bundle. He wonders what everyone who thinks he is doing so great would think if they saw him now, huddled on the couch with chores beckoning to him. He remembers he tells himself he doesn't have the luxury to care about appearances anymore.

Being lonely is hard. Being a caretaker is exhausting.

Being the man he wants to be, well is that even possible? Some days he thrives. Those days you cannot make him stop. But today, well, today is not a proud day.

He has a head cold. His nose is running, and his stomach is unsettled. There's no one to make a pharmacy run. No one to bring the tissues or make sure he is comfortable. He hasn't been sick as a single person. He is his own caretaker.

In some ways, he is confused. Yesterday was a good day. He checked off some boxes, his daughter had a much-needed day away from home. The man had a good day, a fun day. He used to like fun. It reminded him of "before", that's his code for the days before his wife's sudden death.

Grief stalks him. It is armed to pounce when prey is vulnerable, and it rarely misfires.

He doesn't want sympathy. Others have it worse. He doesn't need or want extra assistance. Most days, he seems to manage fine. He just wants an easy day, a break from that overwhelming wave of feeling overwhelmed.

His daughter is unsettled, bored, agitated. So, they make a run to a drive-through. She wants a smoothie, pina colada flavored. He pulls in. They don't have that flavor. She screams and starts yelling for foods that aren't drive-through accessible, much less blended into smoothies. The girl at the drive-through window doesn't understand. The man envies her naivete.

As meltdowns go, he gives this one about a five-out-of-ten. She had an eight the day before in a grocery store and he is bothered that he now scores them. He tries to calm the situation, but neither of them is truly engaged in his efforts.

She gets a banana-strawberry smoothie instead. His stomach gurgles. He just wants her to please stop fussing. She doesn't acquiesce. He pulls into a parking spot, taking a moment to think. He gets out of the car and walks a few steps into the grass. He can't believe this is his life.

A few breaths later, they are back in the car. She kind of listens as he talks. He talks about being upset. How she is upset. How he is too. How he can't seem to fix it for either of them, no matter what is tried. He talks about the smoothie. He talks about her school. He talks about their trip next weekend. He talks about moving to a new house one day. She is calmer now. She is huffing, but she can listen; call it multi-tasking. He claims success.

They ride through a neighborhood and he points out houses. She watches. A mother is pushing a baby in a stroller while a teenager washes a car. A runner goes by. A dad chases after a child in a little, foot-powered car. He thinks back to when he was doing those things. It seems he was someone else back then. In a way, he was.

He isn't the same person he was when Madi was growing up. He isn't at all sure who he is now. He hopes to get to see where his journey takes him. His wife, she saw hers end abruptly mid-path and mortality is now not just something that happens to strangers.

Hours later, they sit at home. They have never been closer but in the moment, they feel like strangers. A few feet apart, both fighting their respective battles. Similar but different. Damaged but resilient. Waiting on the next good day. Waiting on the tide to go back out.

Today, he was easy prey. He vows to make himself a tougher target tomorrow. He has to. That load isn't going to carry itself.

Besides, who knows what the day will bring ... perhaps even a pina colada.

They are sitting alone in a hospital room. The man is with his daughter who is having out-patient surgery. Someone enters. Dad answers all the medical history questions. Then someone else enters and asks the same questions again. He is patient. These are questions he knows the answers to.

Her mother has, or had, heart disease, he answers. He discusses her autism, the best way to communicate with her. He mentions her history of seizures. They have lots of questions. He has grown accustomed to answering them alone.

For 18 years, someone else always answered these questions about his daughter. For the past year and a few months, this is one of the tasks he inherited. All things being equal, he'd rather have had a beach house.

Madison is handling the process like a champ. She understands she can't have food or drink on the morning of the surgery. This was explained all week and she is prepared. Her eyes show a nervous energy. Her dad tells her she is strong. He's understating it.

She has demonstrated strength often in their new world. Like many of us, she has struggled a few times along the way. Getting ready for dances, visiting the beach or New Orleans, seeing her dad with a date ... all difficult for her. All understandable.

They have both come so far. The months have rolled away so quickly. Despite his fish out of water life, he has found his rhythm. He does hair and makeup, shaves legs, endures meltdowns, shops for girl clothes and makes sure she has what she needs. They are together almost constantly.

His life changed drastically when that doctor uttered those six tragic words. He has been treading water to stay afloat while he and his support group build his life boat.

This morning, watching Madison handle the surgery prep without the first issue, he is filled with pride. Proud of her maturation, proud of her strength, and yes, proud of how far he has traveled on his journey.

Through the sleepless evenings, the unrelenting demons in his mind, the feeling of utter helplessness, he once hoped that they could handle whatever life has in store.

He thinks back to the Fairhope hospital room where he viewed her body, not yet cold. Still in shock, he said the only thing he knew to say at that moment.

"Hannah, I'm so sorry. Just so sorry. I can't believe this. All I can say is I promise to take care of Madi. I will do the best I can. We will get through this, somehow."

Today, they are in a hospital under much difference conditions. There's no shock. There's calm, clarity.

"You would be so impressed by your daughter today," he says aloud to the empty chair beside him. "You always gave her so much love. Even in your final moments, your thoughts were of taking care of her.

"I hope we have made you proud of us, like I was of you. I've tried to be more supportive as a father, a family member, a friend. There are times when things are really screwed up, but we push through and try to improve. Here lately, we have handled the challenges as well as we can expect.

"Rest easy Love, we got this."

Made in the USA
Columbia, SC
21 December 2018